A Practical Guide to Teaching Mathematics in the Secondary School

**Edited by
Clare Lee, Sue Johnston-Wilder
and Robert Ward-Penny**

Routledge
Taylor & Francis Group

LONDON AND NEW YORK

First published 2013
by Routledge
2 Park Square, Milton Park, Abingdon, Oxon OX14 4RN

Simultaneously published in the USA and Canada
by Routledge
711 Third Avenue, New York, NY 10017

Routledge is an imprint of the Taylor & Francis Group, an informa business

British Library Cataloguing in Publication Data
A catalogue record for this book is available from the British Library

Library of Congress Cataloging in Publication Data
A practical guide to teaching mathematics in the secondary school / edited by Clare Lee, Sue Johnston-Wilder and Robert Ward-Penny.
    p. cm.
    Includes bibliographical references and index.
    1. Mathematics—Study and teaching (Secondary) 2. Mathematics—Study and teaching—Technological innovations. I. Lee, Clare S. II. Johnston-Wilder, Sue. III. Ward-Penny, Robert, 1980–
    QA13.P695 2013
    510.71'2—dc23   2012019300

ISBN: 978–0–415–50820–9 (pbk)
ISBN: 978–0–203–12574–8 (ebk)

Typeset in Palatino and Frutiger
by Swales & Willis Ltd, Exeter, Devon

MIX
Paper from
responsible sources
FSC® C004839

Printed and bound in Great Britain by the MPG Books Group

Contents

A Practical Guide to Teaching Mathematics in the Secondary School

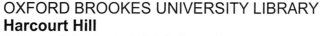
A Practical Gu... ...raight-
forward advic... ...ther in
training or nev... ...able, it
offers a wide ... ...ondary
classrooms. Ea... ...eachers
to reflect on th... ... classrooms, and off... ...further
reading and de...

Illustrated t... ...ssroom
observations a... ...aching,
including:

- managing
- teaching t
- encouragi
- choosing
- using mu
- assessing

A Practical (...ssential
companion to ... *School.*
Written by e... ...ent of
imaginative a... ...ifferent
teaching situat...

Clare Lee lea... ...ity and
works with in-... ...low for
the King's For...

Sue Johnston... ...ck. She
works with PGCE students and in-service teachers in the West Midlands and has
edited many related books.

Robert Ward-Penny is a former PGCE tutor who is currently teaching mathematics
at a secondary school in London.

Routledge Teaching Guides
Series Editors: Susan Capel and Marilyn Leask

These Practical Guides have been designed as companions to Learning to Teach X Subject in the Secondary School. For information on the Routledge Teaching Guides series please visit our website at www.routledge/education.com.

List of illustrations

FIGURES

TABLES

Notes on contributors

Ian Boote is an experienced AST in mathematics who has trained and supported teachers for many years, and is now working as Head of Department in a London school. His interests include the effective use of ICT in the mathematics classroom and functional mathematics.

Chris Chisholm is a Director of Mathematics at a 14–19 school in Leicestershire and a part time doctoral student at the University of Warwick. He has taught the 'Subject Knowledge Enhancement' course for postgraduate students and the 'Student Associate Scheme', a course aimed at giving second and third year undergraduates an experience of teaching. Over the past few years he has led CPD sessions for teachers on a variety of topics both within his school and at local authority level.

Jenni Ingram taught secondary mathematics for seven years before joining the PGCE team at the University of Warwick. Her research interests include language and communication in mathematics classrooms, the use of ICT in teaching and learning, and assessment in mathematics.

Sue Johnston-Wilder is an Associate Professor at the University of Warwick and works with PGCE students and in-service teachers in the West Midlands. She taught mathematics in secondary schools before teaching at King's College London and the Open University. She has worked on several CPD and curriculum development projects including Bowland Mathematics. Her current research interests include mathematical resilience and teachers using ICT to support learning. She has written widely and edited many books including the companion to this book *Learning to Teach Mathematics in the Secondary School.*

Clare Lee currently leads the mathematics PGCE at the Open University after teaching mathematics for over 20 years. She also works extensively with teachers and schools on improving the learning of mathematics and on aspects of formative assessment. She was Research Fellow with the team who researched Assessment for Learning at King's College, London and has published several books including: *Working Inside the Black Box, Assessment for Learning – Putting it into Practice* and *Language for Learning Mathematics*. She has also contributed to and edited several books for both new and experienced teachers of mathematics.

Nick McIvor is an Advanced Skills Teacher of mathematics at St. Marylebone School in Central London. Before qualifying as a teacher in 1996 he had spent nearly 10 years working in theatre and television and in his ongoing work as a trainer draws extensively on that experience. He is now integrating some well-established ideas about performing and story structure with Initial Teacher Training.

Dave Miller spent 11 years teaching mathematics in two comprehensive schools in Staffordshire finishing as a Head of Mathematics. He joined the Education Department of Keele University in 1987 and worked in a variety of roles including Director of Initial Teacher Education for six years. For the last eight years he has concentrated on research into interactive whiteboard use, primarily in secondary mathematics, and leads the Keele University interactive whiteboard research group. He is currently Secretary of the Association of Mathematics Education Teachers.

Mike Ollerton taught mathematics for 24 years before moving to Initial Teacher Education. As a Head of Department he guided his department to teach in mixed-ability groups across the 11–16 age range, using enquiry-based learning approaches. He now works as a freelance consultant alongside primary and secondary teachers both inside their classrooms and at courses and conferences. He is an active member of the ATM where he finds many kindred spirits. Mike has written several books including: *Getting the Buggers to Add Up, The Mathematics Teacher's Handbook, 101+ Ideas for Teaching Mathematics* and *Creating Positive Classrooms*. He continues to be passionate about learning and teaching mathematics.

Andrea Pitt has taught mathematics for many years and was Head of Mathematics in a large secondary school for the last seven years. She is currently a Senior Teaching Fellow at the University of Warwick and is also completing her PhD in Mathematics Education.

Robert Ward-Penny Having previously worked on the secondary PGCE at the University of Warwick, Robert Ward-Penny has recently returned to the mathematics classroom and is now teaching in South London. His interests include the philosophy and politics of mathematics education, and the potential for cross-curricular teaching and learning in the mathematics classroom, about which he has recently written a book: *Cross Curricular Teaching and Learning in the Secondary School . . . Mathematics*.

Series editors' introduction

This practical work book is part of a series of textbooks for student teachers called the *Routledge Teaching Guides*. It complements and extends the popular generic book entitled *Learning to Teach in the Secondary School: A Companion to School Experience*, as well as the subject-specific book *Learning to Teach Mathematics in the Secondary School*. We anticipate that you will want to use this book in conjunction with these other books.

Teaching is rapidly becoming a more research and evidence informed profession. Research and professional evidence about good practice underpins the *Learning to Teach in the Secondary School* series and these practical work books. Both the generic and subject specific books in the *Learning to Teach in the Secondary School* series provide theoretical, research and professional evidence-based advice and guidance to support you as you focus on developing aspects of your teaching or your pupils' learning as you progress through your initial teacher education course and beyond. Although the generic and subject-specific books include some case studies and tasks to help you consider the issues, the practical application of material is not their major focus. That is the role of this book.

This book aims to reinforce your understanding of aspects of your teaching, support you in aspects of your development as a teacher and your teaching and enable you to analyse your success as a teacher in maximising pupils' learning by focusing on practical applications. The practical activities in this book can be used in a number of ways. Some activities are designed to be undertaken by you individually, others as a joint task in pairs and yet others as group work working with, for example, other student teachers or a school or university-based tutor. Your tutor may use the activities with a group of student teachers. The book has been designed so that you can write directly into it.

In England, you have a range of colleagues to support in your classroom. They also provide an additional resource on which you can draw. In any case, you will, of course, need to draw on additional resources to support your development. Other resources are available on a range of websites, including that for *Learning to Teach in the Secondary School: A Companion to School Experience: 5th Edition* (http://cw.routledge.com/textbooks/9780415478724/), which lists key websites for Scotland, Wales, Northern Ireland and England.

We do hope that this practical work book is useful in supporting your development as a teacher. We welcome feedback which can be incorporated into future editions.

Susan Capel
Marilyn Leask
Series Editors

Acknowledgements

We acknowledge with grateful thanks the contributions to this book that have been made by the colleagues, teachers and student teachers that we have had the privilege of working alongside.

We also offer thanks to:

www.teachersdirect.co.uk. for permission to use Quiz Busters Image in Figure 3.3a.

Chris Framer at http://www.CSFsoftware.co.uk for permission to use the Countdown number game image in Figure 3.3b.

Nrich.org for permission to use NRich Geoboard Virtual Manipulative image in Figure 4.1.

Eastmond Publishing Ltd for permission to use screenshot of Autograph 3 in Figure 4.3.

Cabrilog SAS for permission to use Screenshot of Cabri II Plus in Figure 4.4.

The Audacity Team for permission to use an Audacity(R) software Screenshot in Figure 5.1.

Joan Ashley for allowing us to use her photograph of the London Eye.

Tony Lee for support, image editing, reading through and checking, and Rhiannon Lee for ideas.

Abbreviations used

A-Level	Advanced Level– examination taken at 18 years
AS-Level	Advanced Subsidiary Level, the first year of an A-Level course
A2-Level	The second year of an A-Level course
AfL	Assessment for Learning
APP	Assessing Pupils' Progress
ATM	Association of Teachers of Mathematics
BECTa	British Educational Communications and Technology Agency
CPD	Continuing Professional Development
GCSE	General Certificate of Education
ICT	Information and Communication Technology
ITE	Initial Teacher Education (sometimes called ITT – Initial Teacher Training)
IWB	Interactive Whiteboard
MA	Mathematical Association
Ofsted	Office for Standards in Education
PGCE	Post (or Professional) Graduate Certificate in Education
STEP	Sixth Term Entrance Paper

Introduction

Teaching mathematics is both a rewarding and challenging activity. Today's schools, classrooms and curricula offer a huge range of opportunities for going beyond the ordinary, and for introducing children to concepts, relationships and experiences which will equip, inspire and enthuse them. However, the diversity of resources and approaches available to today's mathematics teachers can be daunting, and it can be difficult to know how best to utilise these opportunities as you develop as a teacher.

This book is particularly aimed at student teachers but we hope that it will also be useful to teachers as they continue their careers. It is intended as a collection of practical advice and suggestions which can support you in developing as a teacher of mathematics. Each of the twelve chapters briefly considers just one aspect of teaching mathematics today. The authors have all drawn on their own considerable experience and teaching to offer lots of practical advice and suggestions which you can use in your own classroom. In this way they also draw on the theory and background which is more fully explained in *Learning to Teach Mathematics in the Secondary School* (3rd edition). This companion volume explores the topics and issues raised in this book in more depth, and is recommended here as further reading in the first instance.

Each chapter of this practical workbook can be read as a standalone chapter. There is no need for you to read all of the chapters in order; you should instead think about what you are interested in, and what you are finding problematic in your teaching at the moment. Chapter 1 opens by looking at different ways in which you might plan lessons, and Chapter 2 moves on to looking at assessment for learning, and offers practical advice about how it can become part of your day-to-day teaching. The next three chapters, Chapters 3, 4 and 5 each focus on an aspect of using ICT and digital technologies in the mathematics classroom. Chapter 6 explores how group work can be used to encourage mathematical activity, and Chapter 7 examines how you can develop your pupils' use of discussion and communication to encourage mathematical thinking. Chapter 8 looks at the importance of enquiry and mathematical investigation, whilst Chapters 9 and 10 encourage you to get the pupils out of their seats, so that they spot mathematics in the outside world and get mathematically active. The final two chapters look at your own development: Chapter 11 looks at how expanding your own subject knowledge can support your classroom practice, whilst Chapter 12 introduces the idea of using action research as a professional development tool.

Each chapter contains several *TASKS* which are short thoughtful activities aimed at encouraging you to reflect on the relevance of the text to you as a teacher. You will also find some ideas labelled *NOW TRY THIS.* These will generally take longer to complete as they are designed to take into the classroom, where you can try them out for yourself and consider how the themes of the chapter can become part of your practice.

Every teacher, every class of pupils and every school is different, and you will find that not every suggestion offered will fit your context. You will need to select and possibly tailor the ideas and activities to suit your circumstances and your individual style as a teacher. Nevertheless, the intention of this book is to encourage you to try something new. We hope that you enjoy reading the chapters that we have collected here for you, and also that you enjoy trying out of some of the authors' innovative practical ideas.

Clare Lee, Sue Johnston-Wilder and Robert Ward-Penny
April 2012

Chapter 1 Planning mathematics lessons

ROBERT WARD-PENNY AND CLARE LEE

For an emerging mathematics teacher, planning is fundamental. A good lesson plan can provide a foundation for both effective teaching and successful learning. Planning can also help to tackle many of the concerns and fears that student teachers have during teaching placements; in the words of the author Alan Lakein, 'planning is bringing the future into the present so that you can do something about it now'.

As people think and organise their thoughts in different ways, planning is a personal process. You must develop techniques and habits that support your own teaching, and this chapter is intended to set this process in motion. It contains a number of practical activities which you can use to develop your planning skills whilst on teaching practice. As you read through this chapter, you might find it useful to have to hand a copy of any pro forma documents which your training institution or mentor have provided, and if possible, some examples of lesson plans which you have already written.

BEGINNING TO PLAN

There is no one correct way of planning a lesson. Some student teachers find it useful to sketch out some rough ideas before starting to fill in a formal lesson plan. For instance, you might start with a large piece of paper and write down everything that comes to mind about that concept. You can then pick out the most important aspects for a particular class and draw a path around the ideas (Figure 1.1); this path forms the basis for a more formal lesson plan.

> **Task**
>
> Sketch an informal planning diagram for teaching coordinates, and draw a path through it in a similar manner to Figure 1.1. Do you think you would find this approach useful when starting to plan a lesson?

One of the most common ideas currently used in planning mathematics lessons is the three-part lesson: starter, main and plenary. This is a useful starting point, as it reminds you that pupils' attention spans are limited, and that moving between

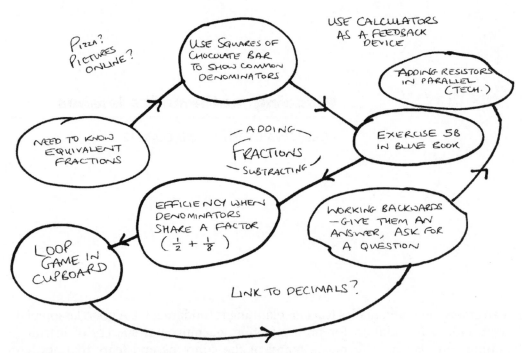

Figure 1.1 Informal planning diagram for 'adding fractions'

tasks can maintain pupils' focus and bolster their learning. However, it is intended as a structure, not a straitjacket; for instance you might find that a longer lesson requires a mini-plenary in the middle, or two iterations of each phase. Similarly, extended work such as investigations may call for a more holistic approach.

Task

Observe a range of experienced teachers and focus on the ways in which they structure their lessons. How do they use or adapt the idea of the three-part lesson? How do they alter the structure of their lessons to suit different classes?

PLANNING EFFECTIVE STARTERS

An opening or introductory activity can serve a number of different roles in a lesson:

- **Linking back** – start a lesson by reflecting together on what your pupils already know. If a class is in the middle of a series of lessons, you might choose to briefly recap the previous lesson. For instance, you might ask pupils to work in groups to create a spider diagram of everything they know now about 'area'. This information can then be added to throughout this and subsequent lessons.
- **Looking forward** – begin with a problem which the pupils cannot yet solve efficiently. For a lesson on the nth terms of sequences, you might start with some simple linear sequences. Can the pupils find the tenth term of each sequence? What about the millionth term? Returning to the same problem at the end of the lesson can help pupils explicitly recognise their own progress and the purpose of the learning.

- **Mental/oral starters** – a good opportunity to develop each pupil's facility with mental mathematics. This might take the form of a generic game such as bingo or 'Countdown', or be tailored to support the learning objectives. For instance, if you were teaching a lesson on straight-line angles you might present a 3×3 grid of numbers, where four pairs of numbers add up to 180 – can the pupils find which number is left over? Similarly, a mental starter on multiplying fractions can support a lesson on tree diagrams and pre-empt difficulties.
- **Real world starters** – a starter involving manipulating numbers drawn from the real world. For example, pupils may work in groups to answer 'how many toilet rolls do you think the UK uses each year?' or 'how many letters do you think fit in a post-box?' and then defend their responses. Questions can also arise from recent headlines or from the calendar, for instance: 'how many gifts were given in total during the song "The Twelve Days of Christmas"?'
- **Focusing starters** – starter activities can also be used to help manage behaviour. Having an activity such as a puzzle ready at the start of a lesson can direct pupils' attention as they enter the room. Pupils could use five minutes at the start of the lesson to work in pairs to see how many playing cards they can make into a stable house, or play a reaction testing game on the interactive whiteboard, generating information to be used later in the lesson. In both cases, pupils who arrive and settle promptly benefit from doing so.

Task

Choose a mathematical topic which you might soon have to teach, for example calculating the mean from a set of discrete data. Which of these types of starter do you think would be most appropriate for this topic? Sketch out two or three ideas for starters which you might like to try for yourself.

Now Try This

Drawing on the ideas offered above, your own ideas and your observations, write down a list of at least five different starter activities. When you are in school, try these out in the classroom and make notes. What worked well? What was less successful, and why? Did any types of activity particularly suit different groups?

PLANNING FOR LEARNING

The *learning objective* is central to planning mathematics lessons. You will usually draw this from a medium- or long-term planning document. However, you should also think about *learning outcomes* in your planning. These will help you to structure and differentiate pupils' learning in more detail. As an example, consider this learning objective: *be able to visualise and use plans and elevations of 3-D objects*. You might choose to deconstruct this objective into three learning outcomes.

Can you:

- identify 3-D shapes when given plans and elevations?
- draw plans and elevations of basic 3-D shapes?
- work with plans and elevations that include hidden (dotted) edges?

This offers a logical structure for progression within the lesson: you might start with a whole-class exercise where the teacher projects plans and elevations of real-world objects onto the board for the pupils to identify; move onto a worksheet with simple 3-D shapes from which the pupils have to draw plans and elevations; conclude with a practical exercise where pupils make a structure with blocks and then sketch the corresponding plan and elevations.

Task

Starting with the learning objective *'understand Pythagoras' theorem and be able to find missing side lengths in right-angled triangles'*, write down a set of outcomes for your pupils that would indicate a clear progression towards a good understanding of and ability to use Pythagoras' Theorem. How might you develop these outcomes into activities for the main part of a lesson?

PLANNING FOR VARIETY

If you ask your pupils what they want from a 'good' lesson they are likely to mention variety, group work and choice. It can be challenging for a new teacher to plan for variety, since transitions can be difficult stages to manage. One rule of thumb is to change the activity roughly every 15 to 25 minutes, unless what the pupils are doing demands more time. Signal the change before it happens, for example by saying 'in 5 minutes I will want you to put those blocks away and get some spotty paper' or using something like a countdown clock on your interactive whiteboard to keep both you and the pupils to time.

Variety in lessons involves a balancing act between several aims. For example, you will need to balance:

- giving your pupils time to build their understanding of mathematical concepts *with* setting aside time for consolidation and practice;
- encouraging the pupils to think and reflect individually *and* allowing them to talk through ideas with others;
- providing ways for your pupils to see, feel and touch *with* requiring them to read diagrams and develop their ability to visualise.

Task

Think back over several lessons that you have observed or taught and think about the ways that pupils worked in those lessons.

It is likely that many of your lessons so far have included individual work using textbooks or worksheets, partly because that is the way mathematics has been taught in the past, but also because that might feel safe while you learn to keep control in your classes. The chapters in this book are full of practical suggestions which can help you introduce variety into your teaching. However, you can also vary the way in which you use the textbook itself.

MAKING THE MOST OF TEXTBOOKS

Textbooks are a common feature of mathematics classrooms, and they can be a valuable source of practice material. Over time, however, pupils will tire of simply working through lengthy exercises, so it is worth considering different ways in which you might plan to use a textbook.

- **Not every question** – which questions do learners need to attempt to work towards the learning outcome? Would it suffice to only do the odd questions, or the prime numbered questions? Perhaps the pupils could decide how confident they are and choose themselves, for instance, selecting five questions from a set of ten.
- **Reverse engineering** – start by considering with the pupils how the questions are graded. What makes question 2f ($a^2b \times ab^2$) more challenging than question 1d ($a^2b^3 \times a^4b^2$)? Where do they think most people will make mistakes? Which question is the hardest, and why?
- **Do it yourself** – get the pupils to write a textbook page for themselves. How will they introduce the topic? Will they include examples? What questions will they include, and why?

Many modern textbook series come with teachers' guides and linked multi-media resources. These might also provide you with ideas to support your planning.

Task

Find a mathematics textbook and choose a page at random. What do you think are the strengths and weaknesses of this page? If you were planning to use this in the classroom, how might you adapt it?

PLANNING APPROPRIATE PLENARIES

Plenaries do not just happen at the end of a lesson! The intention of the plenary is to focus and consolidate pupils' learning, although just as with the starter activity, it is possible to reach this goal in many ways.

- **What can you do now that you couldn't at the start of the lesson?** – you might tie this in to the starter (see 'looking forward' above) or end by looking at a question which the pupils can now attempt.
- **Coming soon** – look ahead to the next lesson or section of the lesson. You might even set this up as a challenge; if you've just looked at linear sequences, offer the pupils a quadratic sequence and challenge them to find and justify the next three terms by the start of next lesson.
- **Why does this matter?** – an excellent opportunity for exploring the relevance of mathematics in the wider world. For instance, you might finish off a lesson on formulae by looking at formulae that pupils have already met in science and technology lessons, or conclude a lesson on probability by looking at the national lottery.

- **Pupil-led plenaries** – occasionally ask pupils to prepare a one-minute presentation about what they think they have learnt. Another version of this is to hide the learning objective at the start of the lesson and ask pupils to guess what it was at the end of the lesson. This type of activity can promote reflection in your pupils as well as giving you feedback on your own teaching.
- **Plenary games** – finish the lesson with a game where the pupils are required to use the skills they have just developed. For instance, a lesson on coordinates could end with a consolidating game of 'battleships'.

Now Try This

When you are in school, try each of these approaches at least once. What other ideas have you come across for focusing and consolidating pupils' learning at the end of a lesson?

PLANNING TIMINGS

We have now discussed a range of activities that can make up the starter, main and plenary parts of a lesson. Whatever activities you choose, timing is crucial. Some teachers find it easier to write actual times, such as 10:15 a.m. on their plans, rather than the timings of activities. This allows them to quickly check their progress during the lesson. Another tip is to plan a 'trapdoor' for each lesson; identify in advance one activity which you can drop without interrupting the flow of the learning. It is also worth having an 'extra' or extension activity planned in case the pupils work much more quickly than you expect, or your use of Assessment for Learning shows that you need to move the pupils on more quickly than you had anticipated.

Once your activities and timings are in place, it is worth adding in some more details. What resources do you need to prepare in advance? If you have a teaching assistant, how are you going to direct them? If you are going to explain a new mathematical concept, what misconceptions are likely to arise, and how will you address them? If you are going to demonstrate a mathematical procedure or technique, do you have plenty of examples pre-prepared? This list is far from complete and might already seem daunting but considering these sorts of issues at the planning stage can forestall problems and make the practice of teaching much easier. It is also valuable to consider in advance how you are going to 'signpost' the lesson for the pupils.

SIGNPOSTING

Sometimes pupils can appear to be involved in a sort of magical mystery tour, where one thing just follows another and there are no clues to help them know what they will learn from what they do. Signposting helps the pupils understand why they should concentrate on an activity and what they will learn by doing so. It sets out the direction of the lesson by looking back to what has happened and achieved before; showing the pupils where they are now and looking forward to what will happen next, or pointing towards alternative routes.

For example, after a first activity you might restate the learning intention, ask the pupils to reflect briefly on their learning from the activity and then say what is to be done next. 'Signpost' moments allow you to give pupils timings for different parts of the lesson, so that pupils can plan how they use their own time to maximise their learning. Good signposting will encourage pupils to be able to say: 'we've just spent time doing . . . in order to . . . now I'm . . .'

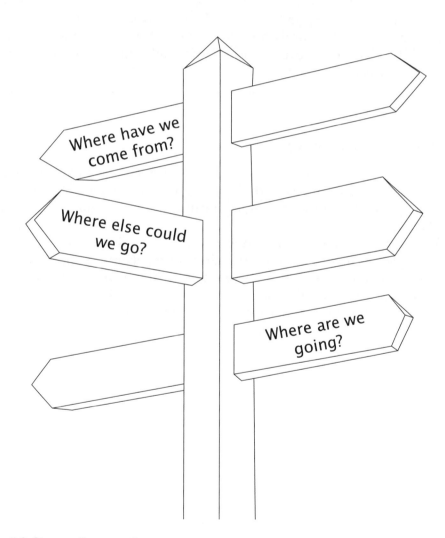

Figure 1.2 Signposting questions

PLANNING HOMEWORK

Homework is a valuable part of the learning process which should not be wasted. It is worth spending some time while on school placement experimenting with different types of homework activities. After a lesson on circle theorems, for instance, you might ask the pupils to write two exam-style questions on a piece of A4 paper with the answers on the back. This could form the basis of the starter for the next lesson, where pupils could swap the sheets and see if they come up with the same answers. Alternatively, you might change the form of presentation involved in the homework. Could the pupils produce an ICT presentation or a poster for homework? You might even experiment with essay-style responses to a mathematics lesson, such as 'write half a page on how decimals are used in the real-world'.

Now Try This

Try setting an 'unusual' homework task, making sure that your expectations for the task are clear to the pupils. After the homework is submitted, you might like to discuss with the pupils how they feel about the different types of homework they are set by each subject. How might their comments inform your future practice?

INTERROGATING YOUR PLAN

At this point of the planning process you will have written down ideas: for a range of activities, suggested timings and signposts and any other notes which are individual to your class. However, before finishing it is worth going over the plan and checking it.

Checking your plan allows you to know that it is as good as it can be. You could consider the *types of activity* involved. At each stage, what are the pupils doing and what is the teacher doing? Are the pupils are simply sitting and listening for a long time, do you need to plan other activities to promote variety? Another way of interrogating a plan is to consider the *types of thinking* involved. Are the pupils simply practising a single technique throughout the lesson, or is there space for creative or higher-order thought?

Read through your plan as if you were a particular pupil or group of pupils. How would you respond to this lesson if you were:

- an introverted pupil with low self-confidence?
- a high attaining pupil who completes written work quickly?
- a pupil who cannot concentrate for long periods of time?
- a pupil who struggles to draw charts and diagrams neatly?

You will undoubtedly be able to think of more 'types' of pupils to add to this list. Make sure that your plan takes account of any relevant special educational needs, and addresses any behavioural concerns; if you were a pupil who got bored and disrupted lessons, at which point of the lesson would you be most likely to cause trouble? Finally, if you are a student teacher and have been set any specific targets by your mentor, it is worth interrogating the plan to ensure that you have integrated opportunities to show how you are addressing those targets.

If possible, look back at a lesson plan that you have previously written. Is there sufficient variety in the types of activity planned? Did you integrate different types of thinking? If you have already taught this lesson, does reading through the plan as if you were a pupil help you understand why different parts of the lesson were more or less successful?

PLANNING TO EVALUATE AND IMPROVE

It is easy to neglect lesson evaluations when you are working in school, as they seem less immediately pressing than many other jobs. However, failing to learn from bad lessons may doom you to repeat them, whilst you will also want to fix the good ideas in your mind. Evaluation can also help you manage personal challenges; it is much more productive to identify problem areas to be developed than to simply label the lesson 'bad' and move on.

Start your evaluation by focusing on the learners. Did the learners achieve the objectives of the lesson? How do you know? If a large enough number of learners did not meet the objective, you might decide to use a different approach or explanation in a subsequent lesson. If all of the learners achieved the objective of the lesson, you might need to consider the level of challenge and the pace of lessons for this group.

You should also evaluate your own choices. Which parts of the lesson went well? Can you explain why they went well? Can this approach be used elsewhere, or developed further? Equally, which parts of the lesson were not as successful? If you were to teach this lesson again, what would you change? How could you support your answers with evidence?

Finally, make sure that you keep a record of ideas that work well. You might find it useful to start a notebook of successful starter and plenary ideas, drawing on your colleagues' experiences as well as your own. Some teachers keep lessons which they know have worked particularly well for them in the past, so that they build up a library of resources and outline plans which can be adapted year after year.

This chapter has offered you a number of tools and techniques which you might choose to use in your planning and evaluation. It is now your responsibility to select and develop methods which work for you. Proper planning can prevent poor performance; excellent planning can help a lesson shine.

SUMMARY

In this chapter we invited you to think about the process of constructing a lesson plan and discussed a number of elements that can be used:

- using diagrams to define the overall lesson structure;
- observing structures used by experienced teachers;
- the use of 'effective starters' for each lesson;
- defining the learning outcomes;
- thinking about variety and the use of plenaries;
- thinking about timing and signposting;
- including homework in the plan;
- interrogating, evaluating and improving.

Chapter 2 Practical Assessment for Learning

CLARE LEE

The first and most important thing to say about 'Assessment for Learning' is that it is not a set of techniques or recipes but rather a way of thinking. If you are using 'traffic lights' or drawing names out of a pot in order to choose who answers a question, you may or may not be using assessment *for* learning. Assessment for Learning (AfL) involves both you and your pupils knowing what they need to learn, establishing how well the pupils are learning from any activities they engage in and modifying learning plans in order to increase that learning. In fact Perrenoud (1998) stated that when AfL is truly in place it will seem to disappear as teacher and learner move together towards enhanced learning. Therefore AfL is not a series of add-on ideas, but is fundamental to every lesson. As teaching has historically often been 'done to' learners, as a student teacher you may not have a series of ideas from your own experience which will enable you to implement the principles of AfL. Therefore this chapter sets out to provide some practical ideas for increasing Assessment for Learning in your classroom.

Developing the way of thinking that is Assessment for Learning demands that for every lesson you:

- find out about what learning your pupils are likely to bring to the lesson and how you will check that they do bring that learning;
- decide what your pupils need to learn during the lesson and how you will let them know;
- know how they, and therefore you, will recognise if they have been successful in that learning;
- check how learning is proceeding on a regular basis and modify your plans if and as necessary;
- consider how they might receive feedback that will help them to continue to learn; and
- strive to be sufficiently flexible to maximise learning for all your pupils.

Each of these aspects works with the others to develop the classroom ethos that characterises AfL: where teachers and pupils are working together in a quest to improve pupils' mathematical knowledge. However for convenience each will be considered in turn.

FINDING OUT WHAT LEARNING YOUR PUPILS BRING TO THE LESSON

Assessing prior learning is a very important part of teaching; you do not have the time, nor is it a good idea, to attempt to teach your pupils ideas they already know. Part of making decisions about this will involve looking at data, but this will often not tell you a great deal. Knowing that a pupil is 'working at Level 5' can mean so many things. Is she good at data handling but finding algebra difficult? Or possibly the other way round? No matter what data is recorded the information it gives will only tell you about generalities, and for teaching you need much more fine-grained information. Therefore at the start of each and every topic that you teach, use an activity that will give you sufficient information to plan to teach the class new mathematics and not to tell them what they already know. You could:

- use mind mapping – on a mini whiteboard or an A3 piece of paper. Ask the pupils to work in pairs to complete a mind map of all the words and ideas that they know already associated with the topic in question. They could draw pictures if they cannot remember the exact words. Asking pupils to include pictures, examples of questions or real-life applications will help them explore their knowledge further. Working in pairs means that they can prompt one another to remember ideas that are 'on the tip of their tongue' so that they report more fully on the current state of their knowledge.
- use **KWL** sheets – ask each pupil to write their name and the topic on a sheet of paper and then to divide the sheet into three columns; label the first **K** , the second **W** and the third **L**. Under the first column they should write all the words and ideas they **K**now about the topic you have introduced; in the second they should write things they have heard about and **W**ant to know more about; the third column should be left blank for now, as the pupils can add what they **L**earn to this column later. Collect in the sheets and modify your plans accordingly. Don't forget to include many of the ideas that they want to know about and to ask the pupils to fill in the **L** column after a couple of lessons.
- test them using the 'end of topic' test – if you already have a test that defines what the pupils have to know, understand and do at the end of the time devoted to the topic, then use it at the start of the topic. Make sure that they understand the point is to find out what they can do and what they need to learn, and therefore you don't mind if they cannot answer any of the questions. Ask them to answer it honestly so that you can plan to help them learn what they need to learn. They could just 'traffic light' the questions (red for 'cannot do', amber for 'heard of it but cannot remember', and green for 'can do') rather than answering them in full, in order to let you know what they need to review and what they need to learn.

Each of these ideas will require about 15 minutes of lesson time, but if that is at the beginning of a lesson you will have to be very flexible in how you use the rest of the lesson; you cannot just continue as though you don't have the information the pupils have worked hard to give you. Therefore it is probably best to devote the last 15 minutes of a previous lesson to the ideas above, giving you time to think about what they tell you and plan accordingly.

DECIDING WHAT YOUR STUDENTS NEED TO LEARN DURING THE LESSON AND LETTING THEM KNOW

This may seem, at first, the least complex of the ideas that underpin Assessment for Learning. A suitable scheme of work may have been constructed for your students using the National Curriculum, and this can serve as a natural starting place for establishing what the students need to learn in any lesson. However, a scheme of work can only let you know what you might expect to teach your students. In order to decide what learning you intend to happen in the lesson you will also need to take into account what you have found out about the prior learning of this class, their interests and particular abilities. Once you have all this information you can include the pupils in knowing what the learning intentions are for the lesson.

For example:

- When planning a series of lessons on plotting quadratic graphs from tables you might find you need to spend a lesson revising the manipulation of negative numbers first.
- When teaching linear equations you might find that the pupils have developed a good understanding of one-step equations from previous lessons, and so you need to move on to more complicated equations, or a related rich task (see Chapters 6, 8 and 10 for ideas on rich tasks).

It is crucial when using the principles of AfL that every lesson has a planned learning intention and that the pupils know the lesson will have been planned with a learning intention in mind. What is *not* crucial is to write the learning intention or objective on the board at the start of the lesson. Of course writing the learning intention on the board may be school policy and therefore you will be expected to do this. It is often school policy because having the learning intention on the board demonstrates that the lesson has been planned with a learning intention in mind and enables the teacher to share that intention with the pupils. When the pupils know what they are intended to learn, they will be encouraged to think about their own learning and their progress, which builds good learning habits. However, there will be many lessons where you want the pupils to tell you what the learning intention was at the end of the lesson, or indeed to ask the pupils what they think they have been learning by engaging in a rich task, an activity or problem-solving exercise.

Mathematical learning must not be constrained by the learning intention, which is why I always prefer to use the term 'intention' to 'objective'. It is important that the pupils know that all lessons are intended to enable them to learn more about mathematical ideas and thinking; it is neither important nor reasonable to always expect the learning to exactly fit in with your initial plans.

MAKING SURE YOUR PUPILS, AND THEREFORE YOU, RECOGNISE WHERE AND HOW THEY HAVE SUCCEEDED IN LEARNING

Knowing exactly what you have learnt and how you have been successful builds resilience in learning, and enables pupils to feel good about their learning. They will then be able to continue the struggle to understand and learn to deal with any misconceptions or other barriers to learning. Therefore designing ways to enable pupils to know exactly how successful they are in their learning is important.

- Most lessons or sequences of lessons can have success criteria or learning outcomes which set out how the pupils can measure success for themselves. For example you can draw a good straight-line graph if you:
  - use a sharp pencil and a ruler;
  - are able to work out sufficient appropriate coordinates using a given equation for the graph;
  - draw horizontal and vertical axes and label them at equally spaced intervals, suitably scaled to allow you to show the important features of the graph;
  - join the points with a ruler.
- Most of the above criteria can be broken down further depending on what the class needs to learn about, and of course using ICT software such as Autograph or The Geometers' Sketchpad would help the pupils explore more and learn more about these ideas. 'Working out sufficient appropriate coordinates using a given equation for the graph' could take several lessons, as the pupils learn to recognise how to work out y given x and x given y and what x and y mean in the first place. Success criteria should indicate success for the pupils in any given lesson. Carefully set out success criteria can become assessment criteria both for you in marking work and for the pupils themselves in peer-assessment activities.
- Success criteria can link from one lesson to another; in the above example some pupils may have understood that you need three points to draw a straight line graph, but others may not. Hence some will move next lesson onto thinking about 'where do I need those points to be?' (appropriate coordinates) whilst others continue with understanding 'sufficient coordinates', or even working with linear equations. Lessons that take account of the pupils' success, measured using such criteria, are lessons that the pupils know are built around their needs, and are ultimately lessons that enable all to succeed. You could photocopy the success criteria and ask the pupils to stick them in their books and cross off the ones that have been achieved as they move through the learning episode.
- Success criteria can be applied for the whole class or for individuals and can indicate how the class (or individual) should behave in order to learn successfully. For example, if you want the class to work as a group in order to learn some mathematics you might set out criteria for this.

Now Try This

Pupils can set their own criteria for success and this is a powerful way to help them develop as independent learners and to judge their own success. With a class that is used to using success criteria in lessons, ask the pupils to define what success will mean in a particular lesson. If they forget to include something important you can say so and add it in. Setting out success criteria in this way can take more time than writing success criteria yourself but it helps the pupils learn an important lesson, that they can decide for themselves what success means.

All of these ideas are about helping pupils to guide their own learning effort, to be able to assess what they need to learn and, in the best case scenario, to sort out for themselves how they can best do that. However, they are also very useful for you because they help you:

- plan the lesson. Once you have worked out what success in a particular idea or concept looks like, it becomes easier to choose activities that will enable that success.
- decide what questions to ask. The questions you use in the lesson should be designed to probe pupils' understanding of the criteria.
- know what the pupils have learned and what they are finding difficult, and therefore help you know where to intervene and how.

CHECKING HOW THAT LEARNING IS PROCEEDING ON A REGULAR BASIS

Checking how the pupils' learning is going can be seem simple enough, ask them! However, you will not have time during every lesson to ask each student a probing question. Here are a few suggestions to make sure you gather as much high-quality information as possible.

- Ask a question worth asking and give the pupils time to answer it. It can be easy to be lulled into a false sense of security when everyone seems to be able to answer short, undemanding questions, or when you ask 'do you understand?' and all the pupils nod. The best way for you and the pupils themselves to know whether they understand is to ask a planned and probing question and allow the pupils time to think about it before answering.
- Take five minutes for the pupils to discuss in pairs what they have learned so far in the lesson. Ask them to identify something they feel good about and then something they feel unsure about. Ask two or three pairs what they have learned well and ask for 'hands up' to show if others also feel confident about this aspect. Now ask for 'issues': take two or three answers, again with votes, and then ask if there is anything else that hasn't been mentioned already. Make an obvious note of these 'issues', and if this is the end of the lesson then start the next lesson dealing with the 'issues'.
- Use exit passes. Give each pupil a piece of rough paper and ask them to write an answer to a probing question or what they feel confident about and what they still have issues with or draw a mind map or something that will provide the information you want. The pupils will hand these in as they leave the room. Try giving out the exit passes at the start of the lesson to remind them to think about checking their own learning.

Task

Choose a topic that you will teach in the near future. Think about one or two questions that would probe your pupils' understanding of that topic. Write down these questions so that you can use them to check your pupils' progress when you teach the topic.

The point about these ideas is to get responses from nearly all pupils in the class and for these responses to tell you what you need to know. As a student teacher you will find staying in charge of all the class difficult at times and your attention can easily be consumed by a few pupils, so it is important to plan activities that will enable you to review and respond to all of your pupils without marking all of their books every lesson.

GIVING FEEDBACK THAT WILL HELP YOUR PUPILS CONTINUE TO LEARN

As discussed in the previous section, helping pupils know they are successful learners is vital and the 'ticks' teachers have used for centuries can do that. However, there is more to good feedback than that. Your pupils will learn best if they know where and how they have been successful in their learning *and* how best to continue to be successful. Therefore, effective feedback will let pupils:

- know where and why they have been successful;
- know what to do next to continue to learn and develop their understanding of mathematics;
- have the time and opportunity to act on the advice given.

If books are marked and comments given, but there is no time or requirement to read those comments, then pupils might just glance at them. The best 'improvement advice' requires the pupil to do something. For example, it might suggest that a pupil:

- reads a page in a textbook, tries out some questions and then writes a sentence (with diagrams) on 'what I must not forget to do';
- goes and sits with a given person for five minutes and discusses a particular idea and then returns to their place and records the important ideas discussed, possibly completing some specific questions at home to ensure that they have understood;
- writes three questions (with answers), an easy one, a medium one and a hard one so that they think about the concept as a whole and consolidate their understanding;
- finds the same topic in a more advanced textbook and makes a mind map of the topic they have just learned and where the ideas lead onto next.

All these ideas for 'improvement advice' require at least some lesson time. Acting on individual feedback given through book marking or orally in the lesson should be thought of as one of the many varied learning activities that enable pupils to learn mathematics. If lesson time is not given to acting on feedback then teachers' work in giving comments will be wasted.

Task

Next time you can access some pupils' work, or using some you have available already, write 'two stars and a wish' for about five pupils. That is, for each pupil you will point out two things that they have done well in their work, and perhaps write some 'improvement advice', a wish that they can act on to continue to improve.

BEING SUFFICIENTLY FLEXIBLE TO MAXIMISE LEARNING FOR ALL YOUR PUPILS

Being flexible is probably the single hardest aspect of using Assessment for Learning for student teachers, and even for some experienced teachers. When you ask a question or watch a group of pupils working together you will find something out. You may be lucky and find the respondent to your question understands the idea you have just explained and therefore you can carry on with your next planned activity. However, what if the question reveals that the respondent has no clue what you are asking or is fully conversant with both the ideas you have just explained and the ones you intended to explain next? You will need to be flexible.

In order to be able to say that you are using AfL you must be prepared to change the subsequent learning activities in light of the information you uncover. You will get used to using your subject knowledge in order to do this, but here are some stand-bys to help out while you build your experience.

1. Ask challenging questions towards the end of the lesson so that you have the time to plan your response. Do this often so that your pupils know you want them to put in some effort in constructing their answers, and so that you can really assess what they need to do next.
2. Have a few copies of several different textbooks available. If a pupil 'doesn't get it' or has 'done all this before at primary school' point them to a suitable textbook and tell them to select explanations to read and questions to do that will help them to move forward. Asking pupils to take responsibility for their own learning is appropriate, providing you support them in doing so. By offering a variety of materials they can choose a layout or explanation that makes sense to them.
3. Ask pupils to work together so that discussion is part of their effort to understand and move forward:
- seating someone who 'sort of gets it' with someone who 'has no idea' can help both of them to broaden their understanding.
- asking pupils who have fully understood the ideas to work together to think about where the ideas could be used 'in real life' or what connections those ideas have with other ideas that they have learned this year; can help to make mathematics more interesting and engaging.
4. Ask the pupils to work in pairs to write an easy, medium and a hard question. This requires pupils to work at their own level, and then to extend their understanding. Ask the pairs to swap their questions with another pair; the second pair will complete the questions and then the group of four should discuss the answers. Then, as a class, discuss what made a 'good' question in this topic, then go on to discuss what issues the pupils still have. Sort out any issues you can there and then or use them when planning the next lesson.

Now Try This

Find a class list of pupils that you know well. Pair up the pupils as 'learning buddies', choosing pupils who can help one another out; these should not be people they normally sit with. Tell the pupils who their 'buddies' are and say that if they are stuck they should go and discuss their work with their 'buddy' before asking for help from you as teacher. You could use this idea for a 'rich' activity such as those in Chapters 6, 8 and 10. Try this out over a period of two weeks. Reflect on how well this works for the class and whether you want to extend this way of working.

You will notice that most of these ideas require your pupils to work collaboratively to help one another continue to move forward with their learning. This is important. Many teachers, especially when they start, think that they are the only one in the room who knows what to do. Most people find learning with one another the best way to improve and you should make use of this in the classroom. Activating the pupils as learning resources for one another means there will always be someone available to help if a pupil gets stuck and there will be someone for the pupil who is zooming forward to try out ideas with and to challenge those ideas. Research (see, for example, Gartner et al. 1971 and Goodlad and Hirst 1989) has also shown that pupils who explain ideas to others both consolidate the ideas for themselves and deepen their understanding. Any classroom where everyone sits in silence for every lesson is not maximising learning.

SUMMARY

In this chapter you were invited to think about the principles of Assessment for Learning and how to introduce those principles into your lessons. The ideas discussed included:

- what Assessment for Learning is and what it is not;
- how to find out about your pupils' prior learning;
- deciding on what your pupils need to learn during the lesson and how you can let them know;
- how you and your pupils can recognise if they have been successful in their learning;
- checking how that learning is proceeding on a regular basis;
- providing feedback that will help pupils continue to learn;
- approaches that can allow you to be sufficiently flexible to maximise learning for all your pupils.

FURTHER READING

Lee, C. (2006) *Language for Learning Mathematics: Assessment for Learning in Practice*, Maidenhead, UK: Open University Press.
Black, P., Harrison, C., Lee, C., Marshall, B. and Wiliam, D. (2004) *Working Inside the Black Box*, London: GL Assessment.

Chapter 3   ICT from the front of the class

IAN BOOTE

Interactive whiteboards are now common features of mathematics classrooms and used by many teachers on a regular basis. A BECTA survey conducted in 2007 found interactive whiteboards in 98 per cent of schools and an average number of 22 per school. This figure has undoubtedly increased; if you walk around a school today you will probably see many interactive whiteboards, as well as newer compatible technologies such as interactive voting pads (see below).

This chapter will explore the use of the interactive whiteboard, not as a gimmick, but as a tool to enhance your pupils' mathematics learning. It will offer you a range of ideas which might help you get the most out of using ICT with the whole class, and help you critique and select from the plethora of resources available.

USING PRESENTATION SOFTWARE IN THE MATHEMATICS CLASSROOM

In many classrooms the use of ICT has been based around the projection of information and illustrations using presentation software such as Microsoft PowerPoint. However, when you reflect on it, a static, largely text-based presentation is unlikely to excite pupils even if it helps you to remember points in your lessons. Presentations in mathematics lessons can often benefit from having an interactive element, or starting with a 'hook' that could help to engage the pupils' thinking. You might begin a lesson on lowest common multiples by displaying an animation of the solar system in motion as the pupils enter the room; this would encourage them to start thinking about what mathematics might be involved in the lesson whilst also allowing you to connect the idea of the lowest common multiple to the alignments of planets. A slide show of images of real-life prisms at the start of a lesson could help the pupils visualise the idea of a constant cross-section.

Many teachers use PowerPoint but do not take full advantages of its features, and it is worth spending some time exploring the options available to you. For instance, *action objects* can be used to make a presentation more interactive. A presentation on the names of quadrilaterals could be set up to include shapes which reveal their correct names when clicked. This would allow the pupils to identify the shapes in any order, which might in turn increase their participation and confidence. *Motion paths* are an excellent way to demonstrate loci to pupils, as you can introduce a scenario to the pupils and then demonstrate how an object would move. Similarly, you could help pupils to visualise the exterior angles of a regular polygon, and to derive the formula, by using a motion path to move a person (or a turtle) around the outside of a shape, showing that they turn through 360 degrees. PowerPoint contains many other useful features, and future versions will continue to offer new ways to make the presentation of mathematical concepts and examples ever more dynamic.

When you are thinking about how to integrate ICT into your lesson, you might find it useful to ask yourself the following questions:

- Is there a way to start the lesson in a visual way? Could you use an animation or video that links the mathematics to a real-life context?
- Would an interactive element consolidate the pupils' learning or just confuse matters?
- Would the interactivity improve the engagement of pupils who sometimes lack focus in lessons?
- What software could you use to create the activity or element you want?

Task

Think of a lesson you have recently taught. What visual element could you have used to welcome the pupils into the room?

Presentation software is a tool for enhancing explanations, not a straightjacket, so it is important that you allow yourself to be flexible, responding to the pupils' feedback and progress. One way of making PowerPoint more flexible and adaptable is to add internal *hyperlinks* that allow you to jump between different sections at speed. If you were teaching a lesson which built on a lesson from a previous year, you could prepare examples so that they were ready, but also integrate hyperlinks so that you could jump to other sections if your pupils understood more quickly or more slowly than you expected. Although this might seem like a lot of work, preparing presentations in this way can allow them to be used for a wider range of classes, and cuts down preparation time in the future.

Task

Take a presentation that you have recently used and add hyperlinks which allow you to jump between the different sections. What would you need to add to the PowerPoint in case the understanding of the pupils was less than you expected? How could you add in further challenges if the pupils understood more quickly than expected?

PREZI

PowerPoint is not the only existing presentation software and other packages are widely available. At the time of writing, one of these, Prezi, is freely available to teachers online at http://prezi.com. If you are willing to invest a little time in learning how to use a new piece of software then Prezi offers you an opportunity to create dynamic and flexible presentations. Presentations created using Prezi store all of their information on one large slide, like a mind map, and the presentation itself follows a user-defined path through the information. This path can skip backwards, forwards and even zoom in and out. Advantages to this style of presentation include being able to move quickly to a different part of the path if the lesson changes course, and being able to focus on either a small part of information or the bigger picture. The dynamic nature of the movement also enlivens the presentation, and you may be surprised by your pupils' reaction.

One good way to use Prezi in the mathematics classroom is to use it to teach geometry. The zoom feature can be used to focus on a small part of the diagram so that pupils can calculate a single missing angle without being distracted by the rest of the diagram (Figures 3.1a and 3.1b). Zooming out can also be used to good effect; you could start by showing your class one corner of a shape and asking them to suggest what the shape could be (Figures 3.2a, 3.2b and 3.2c). Zooming out further allows the pupils to extract more information and refine their guesses.

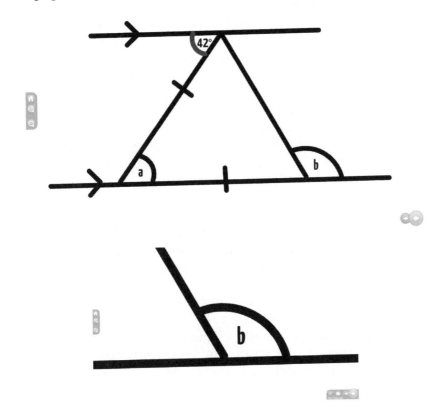

Figures 3.1a and 3.1b Using Prezi with geometry problems.

Figures 3.2a, 3.2b and 3.2c What shape is this?

Task

Sign up to Prezi for free and explore the user-created content already on offer. Try creating a Prezi yourself, adapting a lesson or PowerPoint which you have already created.

BUILT-IN SOFTWARE

Interactive whiteboards usually come with their own built-in software which allows the user to write and manipulate objects on the board. Each make of board has different features built into their software, and getting to grips with these features is an essential part of making the most of your interactive whiteboard.

At present, two of the most popular makes of interactive whiteboard are SMART and Promethean. These two companies' boards can be used interactively in different ways: Promethean boards require the use of a special pen, but SMART boards respond to any form of touch, so a finger can be used to draw or move a pointer around the board. You will probably find yourself using one or both of these types of board during your placements.

With any interactive whiteboard it is worth spending time looking through the included resources libraries and integrated tools. Resource libraries often include backgrounds to enliven your flipcharts, grids for drawing graphs, paper backgrounds including isometric paper, as well as pre-prepared interactive activities which will save you time when designing your lessons. Integrated tools typically include a timer, which you can use to pace your lessons, and tools which are particularly useful in mathematics lessons. Make sure you find out where to find the integrated dice, ruler, protractor and pair of compasses, and that you know how to use them.

The main advantage of using built-in software over presentation software is that it allows objects to be more freely manipulated on the board. For instance, you might set up a selection of images at one side of a page which the pupils could move into place to create a pictogram. The protractor tool can be moved and rotated on the board to model how pupils should be using their physical protractors; in the same way you can demonstrate constructions step by step. Older pupils can move a graph on a background grid, to show the results of different transformations. The built-in software enables you to make the whiteboard truly interactive, and allows the pupils to be involved more in the lesson by doing instead of just watching.

Now Try This

When you have access to interactive whiteboard software set some time aside just to look through the available resource libraries and tools. Choose at least one feature which is new to you, and challenge yourself to use it usefully in a lesson which you are about to teach. Have a look at the SMARTboard (http://www.smarttech.com/gb) or Promethean (http://www.promethean world.com/en-gb) websites and explore the resources that have already been made available there.

UNLOCKING THE POWER OF THE INTERACTIVE WHITEBOARD: SOME IDEAS FOR ACTIVITIES

- Use your interactive whiteboard or projector as a way of turning your classroom into a television game-show studio. Mental tests, topic tests and even examination papers can be turned into an interactive quiz that involves every pupil. A recap on the keywords of a topic could be turned into a 'Quiz Busters' quiz. GCSE or A-level papers can be reimagined as a game of *Who Wants to Be a Millionaire?* Each pupil could be given a set of lettered cards so that they are all involved – some schools even have hand-held voting systems available (see below). These kinds of activities are motivating, as well as being good ways for you to get immediate feedback about the pupils' level of understanding. Templates for game-show quizzes such as these can often be found for free online, and editing these requires very little effort. Another favourite game show is *Countdown* which can be co-opted to help pupils practice their mental arithmetic skills.

Figure 3.3a Quiz Busters. From www.teachers-direct.co.uk

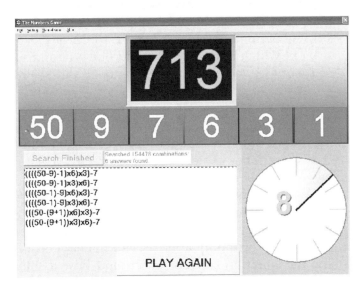

Figure 3.3b The Countdown number game. From http://www.csfsoftware.co.uk/Count_info.htm

- Present the pupils with a matching activity on the interactive whiteboard: perhaps they could match up key words with their definitions, or a set of bracketed algebraic expressions with their expanded forms. Most versions of interactive whiteboard software also allow you set up containers which only allow you to drop certain items into a box. This is a good way for pupils to experiment or test themselves, for instance when deciding which numbers are prime numbers, or when locating items in a Venn diagram.
- Another related matching activity is a Pelmanism game, where two cards are turned over and disappear if they match. Flash templates for this type of game are available on line, and experienced PowerPoint users may be able to create something similar themselves. Younger pupils often appreciate being able to interact with a puzzle like this, and using the timer tool to add a competitive timed element increases interest even further.
- Graph drawing programs allow the class to investigate what happens as constants and coefficients change in an equation. You might start by drawing the graph $y = 5x - 2$ on the board, and then challenge the pupils to type in an equation that is perpendicular but crosses the y-axis at the same point. The use of interactive software allows the pupils to take risks and refine their thinking as they solve the problem. The whiteboard serves as a focus for a class discussion where nothing is recorded and feedback is instantly given as a graph. At the time of writing there are some free graphing applications available online such as the dynamic geometry software Geogebra (http:// www.geogebra.org). There are also a number of more advanced programs available, including Autograph and Omnigraph, which may offer students free access. These usually provide extra interactive features which can be used effectively with A-level groups to illustrate concepts such as gradients, integrals and volumes of revolution.
- Odd-one-out activities can be also be used effectively with an interactive whiteboard. Although tasks like this can lead to different solutions, which can be a good thing, you can start by explaining to the pupils that you are looking for a particular answer, as well as the reason why that item is the odd one. For example, during a lesson on polygons a set of shapes could be set up using PowerPoint, where all apart from one of the shapes are regular. As the pupils click on the shapes only the odd one out will disappear – you can then ask the pupils to suggest why the last shape is unique. A number lesson on factors could start with a set of numbers such as 6, 8, 12, 16, 22, or 2, 5, 6, 7, 11, 13. Can the pupils work out which number is the odd one out, and why? They can then test their theory by tapping on the numbers and seeing which ones disappear.
- There are a number of ready-made activities which many schools have available for use. For instance, the 'Standards Unit' – *Improving Learning in Mathematics* was issued to many schools a few years ago and is still available online. It contains a number of very useful interactive resources. These all come complete with lesson plans and printable resources, although the software can be used independently. Three of the interactive resources from this package which I most enjoy using are:
  - Balance: This software generates some equations, and invites the pupils to complete an operation on the equation to see what happens. The idea is that they see how the equation stays balanced and how a solution could be reached. (This is also available online at http://wirksworthii.nottingham. ac.uk/Improv_Learning_Maths/software/six_applets_FI_May21/balance. html.)

- Building Houses: This provides a 3-D moveable environment where pupils can add and remove blocks and see how this affects the plan and elevation views. The second version of this resource challenges pupils to create structures that match the given plan and elevations. (At present these resources are also available online at http://www.mathsnet.net/geometry/solid/houses1.html and http://mathsnet.net/geometry/solid/houses.html.)
- Traffic: This is an animated applet which shows a car moving along a road and takes images at regular intervals. It demonstrates quite clearly how a distance time graph can be constructed and is excellent for visual learners. Pupils will be able to see how the graph changes when the car slows down or stops completely. (This is also available online at http://wirksworthii.nottingham.ac.uk/Improv_Learning_Maths/software/distance_time_graphs/traffic.htm.)

Now Try This

Ask your department if they have a copy of the Standards Unit box or find it online. Explore the resources available. Try out one activity and share its impact with your peers or the rest of your faculty.

WINDOW TO THE WORLD: USING THE INTERNET TO PROVIDE MOTIVATIONAL CONTEXTS

The internet places a wealth of teaching ideas right at your fingertips. Many of us have used the internet to search for teaching ideas, but you can also use it to demonstrate context to the pupils, and help them to find a purpose behind the mathematics that they are learning; the interactive whiteboard can serve as a window to the wider world. One good example of a free online resource is the satellite view on Google Maps. You could use this to show the plan view of structures such as the Pyramids or the Pentagon. Similarly, you could demonstrate bearings by projecting a satellite image of your local area and drawing over the top. How could you describe getting from the school to the hospital by helicopter? What is the bearing of the football ground from school? Airport runways have numbers written on both ends. For example, the runways at Manchester airport have 05 and 23 written on either end (Figures 3.4a and 3.4b). These are bearings, written to the nearest 10 with the zero removed. By showing the pupils an end of a runway, can they use back-bearings to find the number on the other end?

Many websites offer flash-based resources that can be used in the mathematics classroom to demonstrate many different mathematical ideas. Probability can be demonstrated using random number generators or lottery pickers. Discussions about both theoretical and experimental probability can follow the class picking six lottery numbers and then running a lottery simulator. For instance, if the odds of getting three correct numbers is 1 in 54 and you run the lottery draw one hundred times, how many times might you expect to get three numbers correct? More advanced pupils can interact with a simulated version of the famed 'Monty Hall' problem to see for themselves how it is better to switch doors after a losing door is revealed.

Popular websites like NRich (http://nrich.maths.org) offer flash-based problems for pupils to solve but also free interactive environments that you can use in a number of ways. One good example is their Geoboard environment

Figures 3.4a and 3.4b Numbers on a runway at Manchester Airport. From Google Maps © 2011 Google

(http://nrich.maths.org/2883), which simulates dragging coloured elastic bands around regularly arranged pegs. The board can be altered to be circular, square or isometric and you can also select the number of pegs. This can then lead onto a number of different geometric challenges and problems: How many different triangles can you create on a three by three board? How many different cyclic quadrilaterals can you create on a 9-pin circular geoboard? What do you notice about the opposite angles? How many squares can you make on an n by n square geoboard?

There are many other sources for interactive ICT resources and a quick search on the internet will bring up a whole selection for you to try. However, you need to be critical in your selection, so you should always consider the following when looking at new resources:

- Is the resource clear to see and easy to use by all pupils?
- Will the keyboard need to be used and how might this change the dynamic of the classroom?
- Is the resource flexible enough so that pupils can explore their own ideas?

and of course:

- Will the resource work on the school's ICT network?

ADDITIONAL TECHNOLOGIES

Some schools may have access to other pieces of technology which work alongside the interactive whiteboard and allow further interaction. These can offer new and exciting ways to involve pupils in teacher-led ICT.

- Voting pads are small handheld devices that allow pupils to respond individually to tasks and questions. The pads have evolved over recent years from simple multiple-choice voting systems to ones that allow full text entry. The pupil responses are sent wirelessly to the computer at the front of the room, which then presents and summarises the responses. This allows the teacher to see the answers or opinions of the whole class, or to focus on the responses of an individual pupil. Using the pads in this way allows for a quick assessment of prior learning and ensures that every pupil is involved.

- Visualisers are an evolved form of overhead projectors which can be used usefully in the mathematics classroom. They contain cameras and project an image of anything which is placed underneath them. One common use of these is to allow the teacher to share one pupil's work with the whole class. This can stimulate discussions about how a problem was tackled or the setting out of work, and allows a teacher to share good instances of learning, or help to praise specific pupils, as individual work can be displayed quickly and easily. Visualisers are often found in technology departments of schools, as they can be used effectively to capture demonstrations of technical drawing.
- Tablet PCs are now being used in some classrooms as a way of allowing the pupils to send input to the interactive whiteboard from their seats. Anything written on the tablet can be displayed on the board; a tablet PC can also allow the teacher to teach from anywhere in the classroom.

Task

Investigate what technologies your school has to offer, both inside and outside of the mathematics department. Observe a lesson where these technologies are being used and think of a way you could use them in a lesson.

SUMMARY

This chapter has discussed how using ICT at the front of the classroom can allow pupils to connect with their learning in a different way, and encourage a greater level of participation and exploration. The effective use of ICT in the mathematics classroom can take many forms, including using:

- PowerPoint to create illustrated, dynamic and flexible presentations;
- alternative presentation software, such as Prezi;
- the built-in resources and tools of your interactive whiteboard;
- activities such as matching games or 'odd one out';
- existing resources and finding resources online;
- the internet to illustrate contexts and provide motivation;
- additional technologies such as voting pads.

Becoming proficient in ICT can take time, and there will always be new challenges and new opportunities available to you. However, the benefits can be exceptional, and therefore time spent developing your practice in this respect is time well spent. Exploring and using one new activity each week will help you collect a bank of quality resources which you will be able to use for years to come.

Chapter 4   Pupil-led ICT

DAVE MILLER

The previous chapter introduced you to a number of ways in which ICT can be used to inform and enhance the way that mathematical ideas can be presented at the front of the classroom. This chapter will go on to look at how your pupils might use ICT individually or in small groups to enrich their learning.

Most pupils today have a wide-ranging surface knowledge and understanding of how to use digital technologies for their personal use. However, they may not know how to use these technologies to help them learn, understand and apply mathematics. This chapter will introduce you to some activities and resources which might help you to bridge this gap, and enable your pupils to explore mathematics in a fresh and motivating way.

INTRODUCTION

Opportunities for using pupil-led ICT can grow out of two questions: "How could this piece of software (or hardware) enhance my pupils' learning of mathematics?" and "How might my pupils solve this mathematical problem if they could use any tools that they wanted, including ICT?" This second question is particularly relevant today: in the second decade of the twenty-first century it seems appropriate that pupils are introduced to the use of appropriate ICT to solve problems in the classroom, and mathematical problems are often well suited to such exploration.

However, pupils do not always use ICT effectively in all subjects; for example, Ofsted (2008) found that pupil use of ICT had actually decreased between 2002 and 2007. This is a consequence of a number of factors, but one major reason is that teachers are often unaware of what digital technologies can do for mathematics learning; they are what Dubin (1962) terms 'unconsciously incompetent'. Once you know about ICT opportunities you become 'consciously incompetent', but it is only through trial and experience that you will become 'consciously competent'. To this end I encourage you to read this chapter with an open mind, trying out the ideas, collaborating with others, swapping ideas and resources and maintaining a constant dialogue about what works for you. The rest of this chapter will use the Skills, Pedagogy, Opportunity, Reflection and Evolution (SPORE) approach (Miller et al. 2008) to help you devise, deliver and develop lessons where the pupils are in charge of the ICT.

Before you continue reading, make one list of any pupil-led ICT activities that you would already feel confident and competent managing in the classroom and a second list of any which you already know you would like to learn more about. You might draw on your own experience of using technology in school, ideas you have read about or lessons that you have observed. Have these lists to hand as you read through this chapter, so that you can continue to add to them.

PLANNING TO INCREASE YOUR PUPILS' COMPETENCE WITH ICT

Unless you are at a school that has already started to encourage its pupils to use ICT as a tool to solve mathematics problems, you may need to think in terms of a long-term plan, introducing a succession of activities to enable your pupils to become consciously competent users of ICT in mathematics lessons. Each activity should pose a greater level of challenge and difficulty to the pupils as they become competent in using ICT. For instance, you might move through the following activities:

- **Using a virtual manipulative** – exploring mathematical concepts or patterns using a self-contained applet or flash program;
- **Using spreadsheets** – extending sequences, representing data, choosing and constructing graphs and other diagrams;
- **Using specialist mathematics software** – drawing graphs of functions and dynamic geometric imagery with programs designed with the mathematics classroom in mind;
- **Pupils programming for themselves** – using languages such as MswLogo and Scratch to explore structure, logical commands and mathematical aspects of computer science.

The remainder of this chapter will explore each of these activities in more detail. However, your context will also impact on your choices in this area. Most schools will have internet access and spreadsheet software, but fewer schools will have all of the specialist packages described. Even if you have access to a class set of laptops or a computer room, there might be restrictions about booking these resources at particular times or for particular classes.

As you move through this chapter you should also keep in mind how best to plan and carry out ICT activities in the mathematics classroom. The section 'being prepared' will discuss this in more detail, but generally it is good practice when you start with activities that use these digital technologies to have at least one ready-made file available for your pupils to use, and paper or video instructions. To help you with this you might want to save any notes or files you make as you work through these activities for yourself.

PUPILS USING DIGITAL TECHNOLOGIES

Virtual manipulatives

One of the easiest ways to have pupils take the lead in using ICT is to have them some explore some mathematics using a virtual manipulative. These normally take the form of a Java or Flash applet which is modelled after an existing physical manipulative such as fraction towers, spinners, or figures of solids, and can be built or integrated into interactive whiteboard software (see previous chapter).

Figure 4.1 shows a virtual manipulative of a 9-pin geoboard available online at http://nrich.maths.org/2883 (At the time of writing, apps of a similar nature are also available for the major smart-phone platforms.) If you had access to a computer room, it would be possible for every pupil to have this manipulative in front of them, and to experiment with making shapes using the virtual elastic bands and pegs.

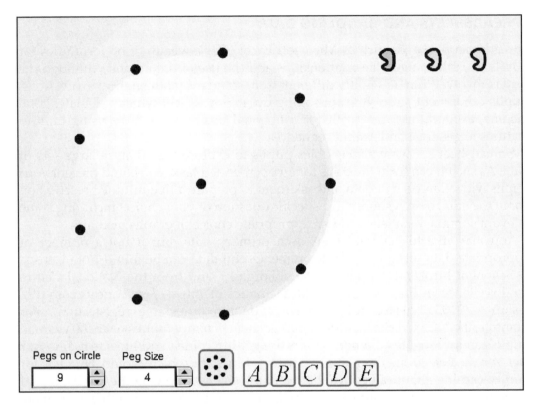

Figure 4.1 NRich geoboard virtual manipulative

Task

Consider the advantages of your pupils individually using a geoboard in an interactive environment over the whole-class discussion in Chapter 3 or the paper and pencil version in Chapter 8. Are there any disadvantages?

Task

Experiment with the other interactive environments available at Nrich.maths.org yourself and then think about how you might plan a lesson enabling your pupils to use one of the ideas that you can find there. Start by thinking about the mathematical questions which the pupils could investigate: What are circle theorems? What happens when you turn two cogs of different sizes? What is the probability of scoring 7 with two dice? Now move onto thinking about the pedagogy of the lesson. What would be the learning objective, and the success criteria of the lesson? Think carefully about what you would expect your pupils to have completed by the end of the lesson, and how you would prefer them to report. What advantages or disadvantages would there be to asking pupils to present their work in a spoken presentation, or via an online presentation which incorporated screenshots?

SPREADSHEETS AND HANDLING DATA

Spreadsheet packages such as Microsoft Excel offer a wealth of opportunities for pupils to explore algebraic relationships and the use of unknowns. Although the syntax involved can be slightly different from standard mathematical expressions, pupils can benefit strongly from setting up a spreadsheet which calculates total income, expenditure and profit for a fictional business, or from using built-in features to generate and extend sequences.

Spreadsheet software also enables pupils to explore and analyse large sets of data. As such it can form the basis for an open-ended task: you could present your pupils with a large set of data and ask them to prepare a five-minute presentation about the data, or in response to a specific question of your choice, including some relevant summary statistics and an appropriate choice of graphs or charts.

You may like to generate your own primary data, but if not a number of appropriate data sets are available online. Useful data can be found from Census at School at http://www.censusatschool.org.uk/ and from the National Centre for Excellence in the Teaching of Mathematics at https://www.ncetm.org.uk/ resources/31033 (please note that some data requires free registration). For example, the NCETM site includes a spreadsheet of temperatures over 100 years so pupils can investigate whether winters are getting colder, and links to a dinosaur fact spreadsheet from the Natural History Museum which would be ideal for pupils learning about categorical data and pie charts. Allowing the pupils to lead through the use of ICT empowers them to select and carry out activities which are meaningful, relevant and interesting.

Task

Using the links suggested or otherwise, search online and download a spreadsheet file of secondary data. Spend 10 to 20 minutes playing with the data yourself; what opportunities does the data present for developing mathematical skills or concepts?

Now Try This

Now consider how you might structure a lesson using this data: would you give the pupils a specific line of enquiry or just ask them to identify a trend or pattern for themselves? How long would the pupils need on this task, and how would you support and monitor their progress? What outcomes would you expect from most pupils, or from a more able pupil? Starting from these questions, plan, teach and evaluate a lesson where your pupils are in control of the ICT.

Some of the data which is available online has already been packaged and presented. A good example of this is the data which can be found in Gapminder at http://www.gapminder.org/ (see Figure 4.2). This site contains a wealth of demographic, economic and political data which your pupils could readily explore. Again, you might ask them to investigate something specific, or just to find and present something which they think is interesting. For an inspiring example of how Gapminder can be used, you might like to begin by looking at, or sharing the short film at http://www.gapminder.org/videos/200-years-that-changed-the-world-bbc/.

SPECIALIST MATHEMATICS SOFTWARE

There are a number of specialist packages available for teaching and learning mathematics. It is impossible to comprehensively describe or even list these programs here, but this part of the chapter will briefly discuss some of those you are most likely to come across in schools at the time of writing.

Software packages including the popular Autograph (http://www.autograph-math.com/) (which also handles statistics) and the free online program Geogebra

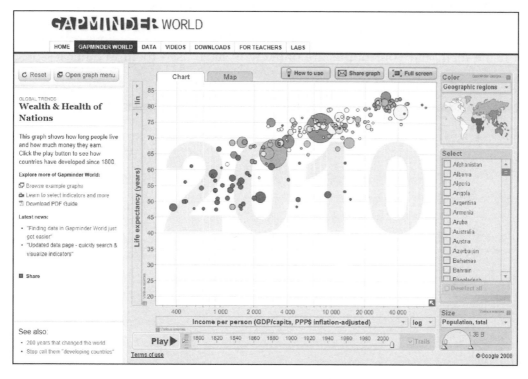

Figure 4.2 Gapminder screen 'Wealth and Health of Nations'. Free material from www.gapminder.org

(http://www.geogebra.org/) (which is also a dynamic geometry package) have been designed so that pupils can easily enter equations and see what their graphs look like. The speed of the feedback given by the computer, together with the chance to delete any mistakes, affords your pupils a much greater degree of freedom to experiment, hypothesise and spot patterns when learning about topics such as the equations of line graphs, transformations of functions, rotations, centres of enlargement, and even 3D-based topics such as volumes of revolution.

You can structure pupils' use of these ICT programs in many ways. For instance you might:

- **Encourage pattern spotting**: use the computer to draw the lines $y = 2x + 1$, $y = 2x + 2$ and $y = 2x + 3$. What do you notice? Make a prediction about the line $y = 2x - 4$ and test it.
- **Set a challenge**: by using what you have learnt about the equations of straight lines, find the equations of four lines which form the outline of a kite.
- **Take advantage of specific features**: use the 'constant controller' feature of Autograph to create an animation which shows what happens to the graph of $y = \sin(ax)$ when you change the value of the constant a.

Other specialist software, such as The Geometer's Sketchpad (http://www. dynamicgeometry.com/) and Cabri-Géomètre (http://www.cabri.com/), is more focused on the construction of geometric figures. These packages can help pupils develop a more rigorous sense of shape, and understand the difference between a drawing and a construction. For instance, instead of asking pupils to draw a particular quadrilateral in their book you might ask them to construct this quadrilateral onscreen, showing that it stays the same shape even when the vertices and sides are moved. These types of packages can also be used effectively to explore topics such as circle theorems, area relationships and tessellation.

At first you may feel less comfortable using specialist packages than the more common spreadsheet software, as you are less likely to have previous experience of using them and your pupils are unlikely to have used them in other lessons.

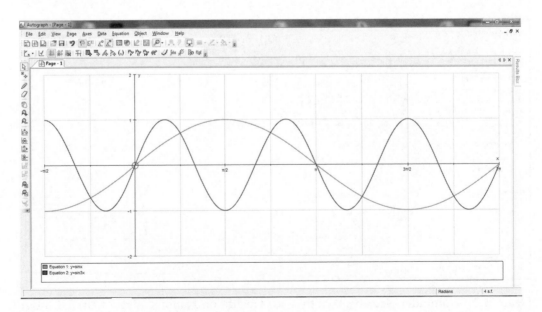

Figure 4.3 Screenshot of Autograph 3

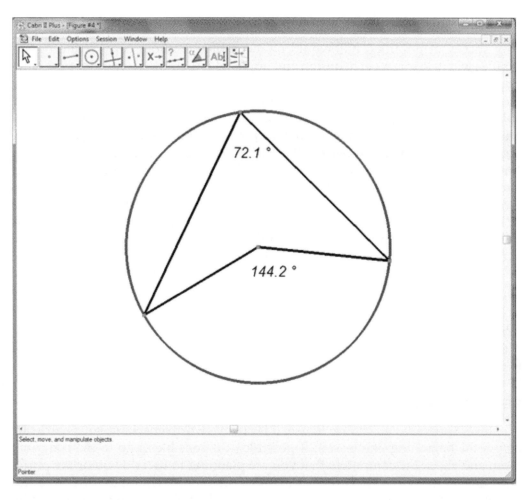

Figure 4.4 Screenshot of Cabri II Plus

However, it is relatively easy to pick up the basic features of most programs and develop your skills over time; furthermore, each of the software packages mentioned here is thoroughly supported with a wide range of documentation and teaching ideas which will help you integrate pupil-led ICT into your lessons.

Task

Choose one of the software packages from those listed above; you might like to choose one that is available for use in your school or one that is available for free (or for a free trial). Set aside at least half an hour and challenge yourself to learn something new; if you are already familiar with the packages, use the online support materials to challenge and stretch yourself. At the end of the hour evaluate your experience. Did you find the software easy to use? What mathematics have you done? What advantages does the software have over a pen and paper approach? What opportunities does this software offer for pupil-led ICT?

PUPILS PROGRAMMING FOR THEMSELVES

Any survey of pupil-led ICT would be incomplete without considering opportunities where learners get to design and implement their own computer programs. Pupils have been learning mathematical ideas through programming for years, most notably through the educational programming language Logo, which can still be found online and in many schools. A number of more modern languages are also available, for example Scratch (http://scratch.mit.edu/). Although teaching and consolidating mathematical concepts through a programming language can seem intimidating, it is an approach which can offer a lot to pupils, as they can embark on open-ended projects which they can direct and take pride in, and thus increasingly gain ownership of the mathematical ideas. You might also find that the ICT department in your school already teaches the pupils the basics of a language; if this is the case you might be able to build on an already existing foundation, or even embark on a cross-curricular project.

There have been a number of initiatives which have tried to encourage pupils to engage with programming whilst still at school, and it is worthwhile searching on the internet to see which organisations and what resources are available to support you if you choose to follow this path. One recent innovation is the Raspberry Pi, a low-cost computer which is intended to promote programming amongst young people.

BEING PREPARED

Whatever software you choose to use, it is always worth checking your hardware before the beginning of a lesson. If possible, it is sensible to go to the computer room and check the computers that you are planning to use: do you or the pupils need any login codes? Do you need to allow time for machines to turn on, or for pupils to find the right webpage? If you are using laptops, do you need to consider power cables, and the related safety issues? Asking questions like these will help you deliver a smoother lesson, as well as helping you decide whether pupils should login to a computer straightaway or listen to your introduction to the task first.

> **Task**
>
> When you are teaching in a school, take a tour of the ICT facilities, and look out for elements which might help or hinder the flow of your lesson. Are the computers arranged to ensure the pupils can also see the front of the room? Does your school have management software (for instance RM Tutor) which allows you to centrally monitor, freeze or share each pupil's computer screen?

Finally, it is unlikely that you will have to devise all of your ICT-based resources from scratch. It is sensible to talk to your colleagues to see how they use ICT to good effect in their lessons, and what books, online resources or shared files are available for you to use. Although each mathematics department has its own way of using digital technologies, you should be able to build on the work of others, whether it is through a comprehensive virtual learning environment, or a scheme of work which identifies potential opportunities for pupil-led ICT.

SUMMARY

This chapter has presented you with a number of ideas of how your pupils could use ICT for themselves to explore mathematical ideas and practice mathematical skills. It has discussed:

- small self-contained programs, or 'virtual manipulatives';
- using spreadsheets to explore sequences and algebraic relationships;
- exploring real-life data sets using spreadsheets and online through websites such as 'Gapminder';
- using graphing programs such as Autograph and Geogebra;
- using geometry-based programs such as Cabri and The Geometer's Sketchpad;
- pupil-friendly programming languages;
- some of the practical concerns associated with pupil-led ICT.

To use any of these opportunities effectively you will need to think carefully about the content and the pedagogy, the mathematics and the management. Depending on your current knowledge the task ahead of you may seem very daunting, but making many small steps leads to great progress.

FURTHER READING

National Centre for Excellence in the Teaching of Mathematics (2010) *Mathematics and Digital Technologies: New Beginnings*, London: National Centre for Excellence in the Teaching of Mathematics. http://bit.ly/ncetmdtreport2

Oldknow, A. and Knights, C. (2011) *Mathematics Education with Digital Technology*, London: Continuum.

Chapter 5   Multimedia technology

CHRIS CHISHOLM

INTRODUCTION

If you speak to pupils in your class, the chances are you will find that many will have smart-phones which can download the latest apps and that the majority will regularly use social networking sites where they upload photos and video on a regular basis. If they are making use of all of this technology outside lessons, then why not make use of their skills in lessons and make learning mathematics more inspiring?

This chapter will look at using multimedia technology in the classroom. It will first consider how you might set up a series of lessons that make use of multimedia technology and result in the production of a mathematical video, a podcast or a screencast. It will then go on to look at some other forms of technology which you might have access to in your mathematics classroom.

LEARNING THROUGH VIDEO-MAKING

Making a video is fun to do and your pupils will probably engage readily with this sort of task. Such activities often help to develop the pupils' literacy skills in mathematics and their teamwork skills too, which make such activities useful in themselves. They also aid the learning of mathematics because:

- they encourage the pupils to really think about the topic;
- they support the pupils in taking an overview of topics and exploring areas where they are uncertain;
- pupils have to communicate with each other about their work and this means that they have to think about explaining clearly what they know, which in turn aids their learning;
- all of these factors mean that the pupils become experts in the concepts that they make a video about;

and

- you have a useful resource to make available to other pupils to use.

Creating a video project can be a little scary as it is necessarily a project that will take some time. Most teachers have used a video camera before, but you may not have any experience in editing video clips into an effective finished product. Many teachers' biggest concern is that they may not be in a position to be able to help the pupils with the technology. What if they asked for help? As you will see, these concerns should not stop you working in this way.

A good starting point is to see what is possible. Start by seeing if, and how many, video cameras are available to you. The mathematics faculty may not own any video cameras but other faculties are likely to have some that you could use. Once you have established the possibility of getting your pupils to produce a video, do a little research. Searching the internet will quickly uncover a wide variety of mathematics videos made by pupils from all around the world. They may range from quadratic formula raps to videos about how calculus is used in real life. There are also examples of professionally made videos such as the 'Maths 4 Real' series made by Channel 4 or those made by Teachers TV (still widely available despite the demise of Teachers TV), which can be a very useful starting point.

> **Task**
>
> Search on YouTube for mathematics videos. Bookmark a few you think are good. Reflect on what it is that you think makes them good.

A project in school

There are several ways to organise a video project in school: a year group could be taken off timetable for one full day to allow the videos to be completed or videos can be completed across a block of timetabled lessons. Planning to complete such a project with at least one other group will mean that there are more people on hand to work with the students, and planning collaboratively often results in a more exciting and more manageable project.

When introducing the project to the pupils, it is a good idea to share some examples of previously made videos in order to help your pupils know what is required and build an understanding of how their video might be constructed. These could be examples from the internet or, once the idea is in place, they can be videos that have been made in previous projects within the school. Then choose a topic that the groups know something about and can research further, and you are ready to begin. Your pupils will need a basic structure in order to get started. A straightforward way that works for most pupils is to use the following sequence:

Section 1: Introduce the topic.
Section 2: Show how the mathematics is used in real life.
Section 3: Give examples of working with the mathematics.
Section 4: Provide a quiz to check the understanding using common misconceptions.

For example, suppose the video was looking at ratio. In section 1 the pupils could introduce what a ratio is, the notation used and how to interpret a ratio. In section 2 they could look at some examples of using ratio in real life; for instance they might first look at making up windscreen fluid for different conditions and then explore how ratios are used in the kitchen. In the third section they could go over some examples of using the mathematical techniques, perhaps using past examination questions. For the final section they could give the viewer a quiz to complete; in my experience questions with a selection of answers to choose from seem to work best. When planning, pupils should think about common misconceptions and make sure the answers given in the quiz challenge these misconceptions.

Now you need to think about the practical arrangements. How many groups are you going to split your class or classes into? Dividing up a class into groups of four or five makes sure that everyone has a distinctive role, but means that more cameras are needed and that there is more to keep track of. Also think about where you are going to allow the pupils to film; the nature of this type of activity means that it is likely that pupils will want to use different venues around the school and outside. The first time you try this, it might be a good idea to complete the filming in a large room or school hall, but pupils can gain a further learning experience if they are allowed to identify and present mathematical situations in the wider school environment. If your pupils are likely to be in different situations around school you will need to consider how they are going to be supervised and how to ensure they are not going to disrupt the learning of others. Could extra learning-support assistance be made available to help you?

Once the pupils have been allocated their topic or theme, and are aware of the practical arrangements, they should draw up a storyboard for their video. This involves creating a summary of what should happen in each scene. This is best done before the pupils start filming, as then you can check that they are not getting too carried away with the story and are remembering to include a sensible amount of mathematics. Pupils can be very inventive about how they go about creating their videos. One of the groups I have worked with was looking at standard form and sent a rocket to space to find the 'Teletubbies' (© Ragdoll Worldwide Limited 1996). As part of this, they worked out the time taken to get to 'Teletubby land' and how much fuel they would need. However, other groups have had a theme but have spent too long thinking about it, resulting in very little time going into actually exploring the mathematics.

A further reason for creating a storyboard is that many groups find that they want to use props in the videos. The art and drama departments can get very annoyed if pupils raid their supplies on the day of filming! By insisting your pupils plan in advance, you give them a chance to locate their own props, which will in turn help to keep your colleagues happy!

Task

Design a storyboard for the topic of ratio. Consider whether to follow the plan on page 42 or to decide on your own structure.

The next stage is the actual filming of the video. It is sensible to check that you are happy using the basic record and playback functions of the camera yourself, but you may find that there are pupils who study media in your groups and they will be able to explain to the class how to use the video cameras and their features. Videos on phones are now surprisingly high quality and in some circumstances you could consider allowing the pupils to use their own phones. Again, make sure the pupils have a plan before anyone hits 'record': in the most successful projects every person knows what their role is and takes it seriously. For example, one person takes control of the filming, another takes on the role of director, another is in charge of any props, and the rest are the actors.

Once all of the scenes have been filmed, it is then time to edit the 'rushes' into a quality video clip. This is often the stage that is most worrying for teachers as they may not be familiar with video-editing software. Again, however, you may find pupils who know exactly what to do and can take the lead. Although specialist software is required for editing, a quick conversation with one of the media teachers can introduce you to the packages they use and how to access them on the school network. This stage of the process can take time, for if you are using analogue cameras they will upload video in real time; this means that an hour of filming takes an hour to upload. It may be best to allow only two or three pupils to be involved with the editing. The others in the group can be set the task of producing worksheets as a follow up to the video. In doing this they must think about the key points of their topic, common errors that pupils make, and how to use the topic in real-life scenarios.

Teachers often have concerns about the amount of time such a project will take. Surely it would be quicker to teach the topics and give the pupils extra time to practise exam questions? However, once the films are complete you will have a bank of resources to use for revision and, perhaps more importantly, groups who make the films become experts in their topic and are able to support pupils in other groups if they encounter difficulties. During the video project pupils will be talking in groups about the mathematical topics they have looked at, creating their own examples and discussing the common errors made by people. They demonstrate to themselves and each other that they understand the topic and can go beyond just following a set of instructions that leads to the correct answer.

Every time you run such a project you will get more confident and feel increasingly able to give the pupils more flexibility to create their own productions. This can be a good way to motivate Year 12 pupils once they return from study leave; for example, dividing the topic of functions, usually taught at the start of Year 13, between groups who then become responsible for teaching those aspects to the rest of the class.

Now Try This

Choose a suitable class and make a revision video on topics you have recently covered.

USING PODCASTING AS A TOOL FOR LEARNING MATHEMATICS

A podcast can be thought of as a radio show that can be recorded and distributed over the internet. It can be saved in different formats so that pupils can listen to it on their own music players. Podcasting allows pupils to record something related to their work and then listen to it at a later date to aid learning and revision. It could be as simple as a recording of the formulae for the area of different shapes or a list of the first fifteen square numbers, or as complicated as a short piece of drama or news report that explains the difference between the mean, mode and median.

The benefits of using podcasts in lessons are similar to those of making a mathematics video. It helps develop literacy skills in mathematics by making pupils think about the best ways of explaining different ideas and concepts so that they are easy to understand without the use of diagrams. It is also a great way of developing teamwork skills and getting pupils to work with people they wouldn't normally work with.

Creating a podcast can be surprisingly simple. All you need is a computer or laptop with an internal or external microphone and suitable software. If your school does not already have something suitable installed on the school network, you will need to speak to your ICT technician. However, you might choose to use 'Audacity', a free piece of software available at http://audacity.sourceforge. net/download/. This type of software enables you to record the podcast and also add in effects, music or jingles.

Any new piece of software can be confusing at first, but software such as Audacity is relatively straightforward to use. In the help menu you will find 'Quick Help', and there is also a manual designed to help you learn the basics of using it. A quick search on the internet will also bring up a variety of different guides.

Once again, you might be surprised by your pupils' facility with this kind of program. There are usually a few pupils in every class who are very quick at learning how to use a new piece of software and will be happy to support other pupils who are having difficulties. It can be a good idea to select a small group of pupils who have already used similar software to become the class's software experts. You might ask for some volunteers, and ask them to download the software at home or access it from the school's Virtual Learning Environment (VLE) and learn how to use it a week before it is to be used in class, so they can support other members of the group. Having this team of experts frees you up to focus on making sure the mathematical content of the podcast is correct.

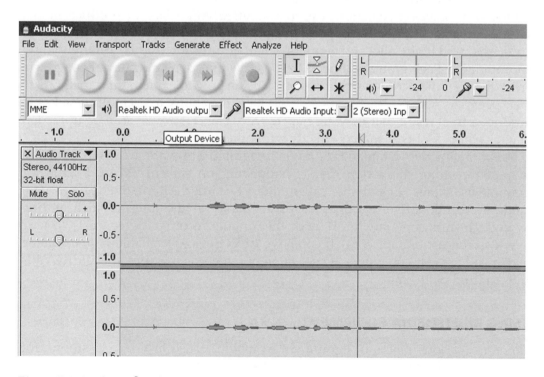

Figure 5.1 Audacity® software screenshot. Audacity® software is copyright © 1999–2012 Audacity Team. The name Audacity® is a registered trademark of Dominic Mazzoni

> **Task**
>
> Download Audacity or a similar piece of software and explore what it can do. Record your own podcast about a topic you have recently taught. Can you work out how to add in jingles?

Once the pupils have recorded their own podcasts they need to be shared. They can usually be placed on the school VLE so they are easily accessible to everyone in the class and possibly other students. I usually give different topics to each group so that by the end of the lesson I have a bank of resources that pupils can use for revision. Pupils have commented that listening to these podcasts on their own music players when walking home from school makes formulae and algorithms much easier to learn!

SCREENCASTING

Another way in which pupils can use multimedia to support their learning of mathematics is screencasting. A screencast consists of the recording of a computer screen output, or the output from an interactive whiteboard, together with an audio track that describes what is going on. You have probably come across examples of screencasting on websites such as Exam Solutions (www.examsolutions.co.uk) or through using commercial products such as Mathswatch (www.mathswatch.co.uk). Since they can be paused or repeated, screencasts are a way of pupils being guided through a question or topic in their own time, and in much the same way as the videos and audio podcasts described above, pupils can benefit from producing their own screencasts to share with each other.

One way of using screencasts is to challenge your class to produce model solutions for an entire exam paper. Split up the paper into questions or pairs of questions, and then allocate them to small groups of pupils, differentiating appropriately. Each group will need to solve the questions they have been given, break their solutions down into steps and decide how to explain their methods to their peers. As with podcasting, the pupils have the ability to do multiple takes to produce a final result that they are happy with. Good examples can be uploaded to your school's VLE or shared directly with other students.

Many interactive whiteboards have integrated software which provides a way of recording the action that is happening on screen: SMARTboards for example use a piece of software called Smart Recorder. Alternatively, there are a range of additional software packages available on the internet such as Jing (www.techsmith.com/jing.html) and the online recorder Screencast-O-Matic (www.screencast-o-matic.com). If you have tablet devices available, a quick online search will present you with a big selection of screencasting apps specific to iPads and Android platforms.

USING MULTIMEDIA EQUIPMENT

There are various pieces of equipment available to use in your classroom, for example the voting machines that were discussed in the previous chapter. The remainder of this chapter will consider some of the types of equipment that are usually available to mathematics departments.

Data loggers

Data loggers are pieces of equipment that automatically collect data on a regular basis; for instance, you might set up a data logger to measure the temperature every hour, or the amount of light on a particular spot once a day. Once activated a data logger can be left unattended to measure and record information for the duration of the monitoring period. This allows for a comprehensive, accurate picture of the environmental conditions being monitored.

Data loggers have been widely available in schools for several years but may need tracking down in your particular school. If you cannot find them in the mathematics department then you may need to visit the science department or the design and technology department. A data logger is generally battery powered, portable, and equipped with a microprocessor, internal memory for data storage, and sensors. The data loggers in school will be designed to interface with the school computer system and there will be software available to activate the data logger and to view and analyse the collected data. Some data loggers have a local interface device (keypad, LCD) and can be used as stand-alone devices. Whatever type is available to you, the object of using this equipment will be to obtain data over a long period of time. The type of data that can be obtained will vary with the sensors available on the data loggers; it is usually possible to measure environmental factors such as relative humidity and noise but other weather factors can be measured and wildlife research is possible.

Data loggers simply log and store data. Their value, therefore, resides in the question that the data answers or the problem for which it provides data. Hence, as with all digital technology, rather than thinking 'I have this device what can I do with it?' it is better to think 'I have this problem. What digital technology or other resources will provide ideas to help me solve it?' Data loggers can provide simple data that will help answer questions such as what is the temperature of a cooling liquid. However, they can also help to answer other types of logistical problems. For example:

- *The local council wants to reduce costs by selling part of the school playing field. How can we persuade them of the value of our fields?* Data loggers could show that noise levels in certain parts of the field are low, providing an area of peace and quiet at break time, and motion sensors could also provide data about the amount of wildlife that is present. A great deal of interpretation will be necessary in order for the pupils to make their case, and this is one of the strengths of using this type of resource.
- *The school needs to save money on heating. What can be done to keep us warm and save money?* Suitably placed data loggers will identify places in the school that are too cold or too hot, and by considering what else may be happening at the time, for example doors left open at break time or people in a room causing it to heat up, the pupils can suggest solutions.

Task

Brainstorm ten different problems that data loggers might be useful in solving. Do not go into detail but push yourself to think widely and find ten. Now pick one and develop it in slightly more detail. Make a note to investigate whether your school has data loggers or if there is somewhere you can borrow them from and consider how they can be used to solve the problem you identified.

Graphic calculators and tablet devices

Another piece of equipment which you might have available to use in the mathematics classroom is the graphic calculator. Graphic calculators have long been a feature of mathematics classrooms, helping pupils to find exact solutions to equations by inspection, visualise graphs and their intersections, and calculate summary statistics. However, modern graphical calculators have an enlarged range of functionality and are increasingly easy to use. Newer calculators display in colour, move cleanly between data, algebra and graphs, and can integrate images and even animations; they can also be connected to input devices such as thermometers and sound-level meters so that they function as data loggers. Graphic calculators can be powerful tools in lessons as they enable pupils to explore graphs or handle data quickly without having to move to a computer; they can even be taken outside to support 'maths on the go'.

Finally, at the time of writing, some schools have class sets of tablet PCs for pupils to use in lessons. Similar to graphic calculators, tablet PCs allow pupils to enhance their mathematics with technology, without requiring them to be parked in front of a desktop computer. However, tablet PCs can also give access to full versions of software packages, including those discussed in Chapter 4; in this way, any room can temporarily become a 'computer room' and any work can be saved and completed later on a standard machine if necessary. Other tablet devices such as iPads offer their own sets of opportunities, and it is going to be interesting to see how widespread tablet devices become in secondary school classrooms over the next decade.

Each school has its own technical inventory, and each of the devices discussed will undoubtedly continue to develop and change in ways that will influence their usefulness in the mathematics classroom. Therefore, it is important that you establish what equipment is present in your own school, research what resources are available to you, and consider how you will manage the use of the equipment so that it supports your pupils' mathematical thinking and exploration.

Now Try This

Find out if your school has access to any class sets of graphical calculators. If possible, teach a lesson to a Key Stage 4 or Key Stage 5 group that involves the pupils drawing a number of graphs, and allow half of the pupils to use graphic calculators. What advantages did these pupils have over their peers? Were there any disadvantages or drawbacks associated with using the graphic calculators? (Note: to be fair to all pupils you may need to spend five or ten minutes at the start of the lesson ensuring that the pupils know how to use the basic functions of the calculator.)

CONCLUSION

All English secondary schools now have a Virtual Learning Environment (VLE) but many of these are currently underused. Most VLEs have the capability for blogging, uploading different formats of files, creating a variety of forums and adding web links, all of which can give pupils access to interactive learning resources 24 hours a day. Learning how to use these technologies to aid learning will be something that can be useful in interesting and engaging your pupils.

> **Task**
>
> Speak to the lead teacher for ICT in your school and find out which faculties use the school VLE most effectively. Have a look at what features they use and think about how these ideas could be adapted for the mathematics department.

This chapter has only touched on some ways in which you can use multimedia in your lessons, but hopefully you have already been inspired to try something new. Whether you are using data loggers for a single lesson, or planning a sequence of lessons leading to a podcast, the most important rule for working with new technologies is not to be afraid of them. Challenge yourself to try out some new equipment or software and, if possible, encourage the pupils to become the experts, as this will allow you to focus on the mathematics and the pupils' learning.

SUMMARY

This chapter has presented you with a number of ideas of how multimedia resources might add to your lessons, but more importantly how they can enable your pupils to use mathematical ideas and practice mathematical skills in new and interesting ways. It has discussed:

- making videos as a way to encourage pupils to explore their mathematical understandings;
- how podcasts can be used as a tool for learning mathematics;
- why working collaboratively in the making of a video or a podcast can improve pupils' literacy and team-working skills at the same time as improving their mathematics;
- using screencasting to help pupils' learning and revision;
- how multimedia resources can be integrated into lessons;
- the ways that multimedia equipment such as data loggers and graphic calculators can be used as added resources in learning mathematics.

To use any of these opportunities effectively you will need to think carefully about the content and the pedagogy, the mathematics and the management. Many of the ideas in this chapter will need detailed and careful planning but they will also lead to involving and challenging learning of mathematical ideas.

Chapter 6   **Working collaboratively**

ANDREA PITT

When I began my teaching career I thought that simply rearranging the classroom, from rows into groups of desks, would ensure that my classes worked together as groups. However, as time went on I came to realise that what was happening in my classroom was that pupils were working individually on the questions I had set, conferring on answers from time to time and then going back to individual work. What was definitely not happing, despite the arrangements of the desks, was any form of collaborative group work. I began to realise that if I wanted my pupils to work in a collaborative way then I had to offer them activities that would require them to do so, and that I needed to help them develop the ways of working together that would enable them to work in a truly collaborative fashion. Moving the tables was only the start!

WHY WORK COLLABORATIVELY?

What benefits does collaborative work offer that other ways of working do not?

Research (for instance, Mercer and Littleton 2007 and Swan 2006) shows that working as a group allows pupils to:

- develop conceptual understanding;
- develop strategies for tackling challenging problems;
- learn how to reason and argue constructively;
- gain feedback so that ideas maybe refined and developed;
- learn how to work with, and learn from others.

The abilities to work in this way, to tackle difficult problems and work collaboratively with others are vital skills for employment in the twenty-first century. Employers no longer need people to act as knowledge bases or to compute large calculations manually, since there are machines to do this for us. What is needed are people to do the thinking, to synthesise information, to interpret and present data, both quantitative and qualitative, and to know how to respond when things do not turn out as expected. This is not something which can develop and flourish in a mathematics classroom where pupils are merely imitating methods demonstrated by the teacher whilst working through textbook exercises. It requires a different way of being in the classroom. Pupils need to be aware of both individual and group goals and how the accountability for these goals is something that is shared by all members of the group. Such a mathematics classroom differs greatly from the model seen in many classrooms where pupils are responsible only for their own learning and where the focus is on obtaining the correct answer.

In order to plan for effective collaborative learning in your classroom you need to give careful consideration to the tasks you offer to pupils, the way you group them and the way you arrange your room in order for this to happen. I will now consider the issues surrounding each of these.

RICH TASKS

In order to encourage pupils to work collaboratively with others they need to be offered tasks that they cannot solve quickly and easily by themselves. This is in contradiction to the way many textbooks are generally set up and how mathematics is often taught. Pupils cannot be expected to invest time and thought into their learning if what they are offered is something that can be solved either by inspection or by following an algorithm given to them by the teacher. Collaborative learning requires a shift from a view of mathematics as something where they work through exercises, towards a recognition that they are working on developing their understanding and the understanding of others in their group. For much of the time it should be the pupils telling the teacher about the mathematics not the other way round! For this to happen they need to be working on rich tasks and difficult problems.

Rich tasks are those which:

- all learners can access;
- offer challenge to all;
- differentiate by outcome;
- need to be thought about, discussed and mulled over;
- enable generalisations and conjectures to be made and tested;
- can be tackled by a variety of approaches and so involve learners in making decisions;
- focus on the journey rather than the answers;
- help learners see the connections within mathematics.

There are organisations such as the ATM and the MA, and resources such as the Standards Unit box, which provide content-specific rich tasks. There are also lots of excellent ideas for tasks in Chapter 8.

The following sections discuss some generic ways of working with groups that can be applied to different content areas.

Card sorts

Pupils can be given sets of cards containing mathematical statements and then be asked to decide if they are always, sometimes or never true. The pupils must provide mathematical reasons and examples or counter examples to justify placing each card in a particular category. An example of a statement might be *the bigger the perimeter of a rectangle, the larger its area* or *the larger the coefficient of x, the steeper the line*. These answers can be portrayed with their reasoning on a poster and presented to the class.

Sets of cards can be designed for pupils to match different representations of the same mathematical idea; for example, a set of three might contain a frequency table, a stem and leaf diagram, and a box and whisker plot, or a mapping diagram, an equation and a graph. Pupils may practise a technique using a jigsaw or matching pairs exercise, for instance following work expanding algebraic brackets pupils might match a statement with its simplified form. The freely available Tarsia software enables sets of cards to be made quickly and easily and is available from http://download.cnet.com/Formulator-Tarsia/3000–2051_4–10584458.html.

Posters

These can be used at the end of a task to summarise what has been understood and to ensure your pupils remember the ideas, or they can be used at the beginning of a task to find out what pupils already know about a topic. Alternatively they can be used as a working document on which pupils work together to solve a problem, explain what they are doing and why. There is something about a large piece of sugar paper that encourages working together!

Writing own questions

Often you will have a stack of textbooks at the back of your room or in a cupboard. Ask groups to look at an exercise and to work on putting the questions in order of difficulty. What makes some questions harder than others? Ask them to write similar but more interesting/challenging questions of their own. Can they write an easy question, a difficult question? What makes the question easy or hard?

Devising a strategy to answer a hard question and comparing different strategies

When using this idea try to tell pupils as little as possible. Give them a difficult question to work on in pairs or groups, then after they have worked for a short while ask them to report back to the class. As each group presents ask the pupils to decide if a strategy will only work in the particular case or is it a general method. Help them see that the power of mathematics is in the generality and get them to describe that generality themselves.

Now Try This

Think about a topic you are going to teach soon. Devise a card jigsaw for pupils to practise the ideas that you will teach. Observe the interaction between pupils as they work together to solve it. Notice what they are saying to each other. Be less helpful; let them work with each other to construct the jigsaw.

HOW TO GROUP PUPILS

When considering how to group pupils you will need to think about the size and the makeup of the groups. How many pupils will you have in each group? How will you allocate pupils to groups? The answers to these questions will vary between classes and tasks and the room you are teaching in. The options for group size could include pairs, threes or fours or larger groups of six to eight and the groups could be based on friendship, attainment, sex or be completely random. The effectiveness of group work in promoting learning depends upon the extent to which learners give and receive help from their peers.

Reflect on a lesson where you used group work. How did you decide on group size and make up? What other choices could you have used? Would they have made the group work more or less effective?

Group size

Pairs: Grouping pupils in pairs is quick and easy to implement and as there are only two members of the group there is an expectation that both will speak and contribute. On the other hand the amount of challenge from different points of view is limited and agreement maybe reached quickly without considering all options or variables.

Small groups: Enlarging the group size allows for diversity of opinion and experiences whilst at the same time the group is small enough for all members to express their views. However, it is possible that a pupil may become passive and allow others to do the work. This is why it is important to ensure that pupils are aware that the group is accountable for the learning of all its members. All members of the group need to understand, as any of them may be called upon to present feedback.

Larger groups: Having slightly larger groups allows for a wider diversity of ideas and opinions. Pupils have to learn how to negotiate a wider range of ideas and develop strategies to enable them to make effective contributions. At times a larger group may split into smaller sub-groups or some pupils may dominate the discussions leaving others feeling disenfranchised. At times you may wish to change the group size as the task develops. You might start with pair work and then ask pupils to discuss in fours and reach a consensus within the new larger group. This could be extended to even larger groups and then to form a whole-class discussion. This way of working is often referred to as a 'snowball approach'.

Task

Think about one of your classes, what would be the advantages and disadvantages of using different group sizes with this particular class? Walk around your school and observe how various group sizes are used by different teachers.

Now Try This

Identify one of your classes that you will teach soon. Plan to use a snowball approach to generate discussion and collaborative working. After the lesson reflect on how the pupils responded to the different group sizes.

Group makeup

Identify a teacher who uses group work effectively; discuss with them how they structure the membership of their groups.

Friendship groups: These often work very well as pupils have already established working relationships and feel at ease discussing things that they find difficult as they do not fear being judged. Pupils are respectful of the feelings of their friends. This is important as research has shown that disrespectful interactions between pupils have a negative effect on attainment. However, groups of friends may not challenge each other and may reach consensus too easily without considering all the options.

Attainment groups: Sitting pupils with others of the same attainment in a class visibly demonstrates in-class setting and can lead to different groups being offered different tasks to work on. This denies pupils equality of opportunity, as the teacher pre-judges the potential attainment of each group. Research clearly shows that ability grouping has negative effects that stretch beyond schooling. It has been demonstrated that groups work best in promoting learning when they are similar, but not homogenous, in attainment. To achieve this, middle attainers should be grouped with high attainers or middle attainers with lower attainers. Grouping high attainers with low attainers often means that the latter group does not contribute effectively to discussions and also it can introduce hierarchies within the group.

Single-sex groups: Separating pupils into single-sex groups can be more comfortable for some learners and can overcome issues such as male dominance of technology. However, it is not reflective of the way in which society works and may result in gender divisions within a classroom.

Random groups: Whilst these may be seen by pupils as a democratic way of forming of groups and they do widen the range of partners that pupils have to work with, you have no control over negating the difficulties outlined above as possible limitations in the different ways of grouping pupils.

Now Try This

Choose one of your classes and, using your assessment of their learning, group them into the type of attainment groups shown by the research to be most effective in promoting learning.

CLASSROOM LAYOUT

The typical layout seen in mathematics classrooms around the country, desks in rows facing the front, is not conducive to collaborative learning. It is difficult for pupils to talk, listen and interact with each other. The focus of the room is the teacher standing at the front, viewed around the back of other people's heads!

> **Task**
>
> Consider the room you teach in. How does the arrangement of the furniture influence the teaching and learning strategies you use? Go for a walk around school and look at the different classroom layouts. What are the pupils doing?

If you want your pupils to experience the benefits of learning collaboratively in your classroom you need to facilitate this by arranging your furniture accordingly. Having your desks in a horseshoe formation can be useful for discussion but it can be difficult for pupils to work in groups other than pairs or as a whole class and movement of the teacher, or the learners, around the classroom maybe constrained. Having desks in blocks allows the flexibility of working in pairs or larger groups and movement around the classroom is relatively easy.

> **Now Try This**
>
> Draw up two or three arrangements of your classroom and consider the advantages and challenges of each. Now select a class that you think will respond well to a new arrangement and choose a lesson to try it out.

THE TEACHER'S ROLE

You have arranged your tables, organised your groups and picked a rich task. Now what is your role as the teacher in the lesson? In some ways this is the hardest part of group work. You, as the teacher, have to let go and allow the pupils to assume control and make decisions about their learning. Learning to be less helpful and to engage with the pupils in a way that encourages them to be active collaborative learners can take time but is essential.

Introducing the task

It is important that your pupils are aware of the purpose of the task that they are being asked to work on. They should know why they are being asked to work together and what the shared goals are. You might say: *In the next few lessons I want you to be finding out what happens when . . . You will be exploring what happens if you change . . . make some conjectures . . . you will be learning how you explain . . .* You will need to explain that it is the journey the group makes that the pupils will learn from, the reasoning and explanations, rather than the group getting to the end quickly. It will also be important to highlight that each member of the group has responsibility for ensuring that they all understand. Telling them at the start that you will pick some members of the group to explain what they have been doing to the rest of the class and that they all have to be able to do this will help your pupils to collaborate appropriately.

Now Try This

Chose an activity for one of your classes. Write down what you will say as an introduction and practise saying these words out loud before using that introduction for the lesson. Evaluate the pupils' response to your introduction.

Allocating roles

When pupils are new to working collaboratively you might find it useful to allocate roles to either the group as a whole or to individuals within the group. For example, you might ask the pupils to decide who will summarise what you have been working on, who will report back to the class, or you may choose to name the pupils responsible for these roles.

Reinforcing ground rules

Working effectively as a group requires certain social skills, such as not talking when others are talking and knowing how to reach consensus. It is part of your role to help pupils develop these skills. Pupils may not be used to working in this way in mathematics and so the first few times you ask them to discuss things, you may find that the discussion is not in the least bit related to the task in hand. They may find it hard to know how to share ideas or how to handle disagreements within the group, or they may be unkind if a mistake is made. You might choose to develop ground rules as a class or you might be explicit in your expectations or you might wait and only intervene if it becomes necessary. Remember that pupils will bring group skills with them from other subjects; you may, however, need to remind them to use these skills.

Task

Think about how you want pupils to work together in your classroom. What is important to you? Will you agree some ground rules in advance with the pupils or will you wait and intervene when necessary?

Listening

Effective group work requires pupils to be discussing, explaining and describing. In order to be able to intervene effectively if and only when necessary you will need to learn to stand back and listen, resisting the temptation to join in. This will provide you with the perfect opportunity to assess what the pupils are learning.

Getting others to help

When pupils get stuck, they need to know that they can learn from each other and from resources such as computers and books that might be in your classroom. Firstly, there are more of them than you, so obtaining help in this way increases learning time. Perhaps more importantly, learning that there are resources other than the teacher that can help them is an important life skill. When someone asks you a question, direct them to one of their peers. If you are always the one who 'gets them unstuck', you will always be the one they ask.

Undoing learned helplessness

For many pupils, their mathematics experience to date has consisted of following a procedure demonstrated by a teacher who then helpfully shows them what to do again if they ask for help (see, for example, Stigler and Hiebert 2009). Who can blame them for assuming that only the teacher can help? This is learned helplessness, which must be unlearned. I can think of many tasks that require some thinking and effort that I would choose to get out of if all I had to do was say 'I'm stuck' and someone came and did it for me – ironing springs to mind here! You should be the one asked for help when they have tried several or even many other strategies, not the first port of call.

> **Task**
>
> Think about how you currently respond when a pupil comes to you and says 'I'm stuck'. Now think about what you might say instead.

Time

Having decided how long a task might take, you might find it useful to help pupils use this time effectively, and when first using group work, reminders about time can help keep them on task. During your introduction to the task you could tell pupils how much time they have before they need to report back and ask them to begin by planning out the time, or you might choose to give out markers. For example, you might tell pupils 'You have 15 minutes left, you need to think about what else needs to be done'.

CONCLUSION

It can take time to develop the skills of cooperative group working and for pupils to realise that you, as the teacher, are not, and should not be, their first port of call when they get stuck. They need to be given time to work on developing the skills required to work collaboratively. For some groups this will take a longer time than for others. Social skills such as listening to and commenting on the views of others may need to be addressed as part of the process. The learning gains are, both in terms of mathematics and in developing the personal qualities and skills required for life in the twenty-first century, proven. For me as a teacher standing in an unobtrusive part of my classroom watching and listening as pupils discuss complex problems, seeing them trying to convince others that they have an idea that is worth exploring, and watching as they get better at learning mathematics, the rewards are immense and far outweigh the difficulties it takes trying to get there. Teaching doesn't get better than this.

SUMMARY

In this chapter you were invited to think about the advantages and disadvantages of asking your class to work collaboratively and the practicalities of setting up group work. These included:

- why working collaboratively can increase the learning that pupils are able to do in your lessons;
- the differences between sitting together in groups and working collaboratively as a group;
- the types of activity that are suitable for use when asking pupils to work in groups;
- how to make choices about the size and structure of the groups you use;
- how to arrange your classroom for group working;
- the role of the teacher when pupils are working in groups.

FURTHER READING

Mercer, N. and Littleton, K. (2007) *Dialogue and the Development of Children's Thinking: A Sociocultural Aapproach*, London: Routledge.

Swan, M. (2006) *Collaborative Learning in Mathematics: A Challenge to Our Beliefs and Practices*, Leicester: National Institute of Adult Continuing Education.

Chapter 7   Discussion and communication

JENNI INGRAM

Discussion and communication are increasingly being recognised as important in teaching and learning mathematics. There is an intimate and complex relationship between thought and language. Pupils learn through a variety of ways of communicating in mathematics classrooms, such as talking, images and writing, and are also assessed using each of these different types of communication. The role of communication is now seen as an essential part of the process of learning mathematics as pupils construct meanings and understanding during their interactions.

Generating and supporting discussions and effective communication with and amongst pupils in mathematics lessons is not easy. When using discussion in your lessons you will have to anticipate, manage and make sense of a range of unpredictable contributions from pupils. It will be important to generate a supportive and safe environment, as the pupils must feel comfortable in offering their ideas and also feel comfortable in disagreeing with what others have said in a constructive way. This is dependent in part on the pupils' social skills but also on the 'ground rules' that you set out and enforce. It can take time to develop the type of environment that fosters good discussion, which will be built on strong and respectful relationships between the teacher and the pupils. This chapter is about developing the conditions for the kinds of discussion and communication that will enable effective learning.

> **Task**
>
> Observe a mathematics lesson and note how often the teacher talks and how often the pupils talk and the nature of this talk. How long are the pupils' answers? Are the pupils remembering facts or procedures, are they explaining their work, or are they conjecturing or justifying? How are technical vocabulary and mathematical phrases used by both the teacher and the pupils?

INITIATING DISCUSSION

Questions and tasks have a vital role in constructing different styles and patterns of interaction. If you want pupils to discuss the mathematics, explain their ideas and to build on each other's contributions, then your initial questions and prompts will have to support and encourage these forms of interaction. This is true whether you are asking a question to the whole class or setting a task for pupils to work in small groups.

One approach is to ask questions to which there are many different possible answers rather that one 'right' answer. For example, you could ask pupils what they see in a particular image such as the one shown in Figure 7.1 or those in Chapter 9 (for example the picture of a fountain forming parabolas). A short video clip or a pattern of numbers can also be used to open up myriad opportunities. The images also do not have to generate different possible answers – a video clip such as the Nicolet or Trevor Fletcher films can also help to generate questions.

Task

Look at the image shown in Figure 7.1. What different shapes can you see?

How many of each shape are there? Try to describe these shapes and where they are to a friend without pointing or gesturing.

Another simple way of initiating a discussion is to ask the pupils to compare and contrast two different representations of solutions to a problem, or to offer a range of possible answers to a problem, some of which may include a commonly made mistake or frequently held misconception. A third idea would be to ask a question that is likely to result in a debate, such as 'what is the smallest (or largest) prime number?' or 'how many handshakes would take place if everyone in this class shook hands with everyone else?'

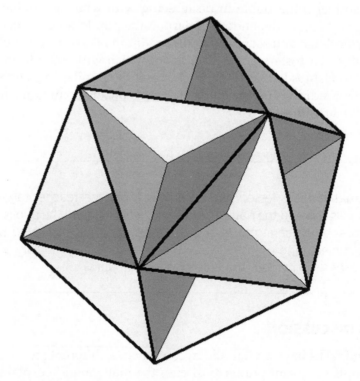

Figure 7.1 The great dodecahedron

Now Try This

Design and use a plenary for a topic you are teaching to generate a debate which sets up the next lesson. For example, in a plenary you might ask the pupils to discuss the difference between 0.9 recurring and 1. This could encourage the pupils to think about infinite decimals and support a subsequent lesson on converting recurring decimals to fractions.

Even if pupils are asked well-thought-out and stimulating questions, they can still be reluctant to offer their ideas and suggestions if they are not used to being asked for them. This is a particular problem in mathematics classrooms where the teacher often evaluates pupils' responses as either right or wrong. Giving pupils the opportunity to talk first in small groups or pairs about a question or problem that has no straightforward right or wrong answer can support them in articulating their ideas to others and develop their confidence to share these to the whole class. This is often called the 'think, pair, share' approach, as pupils are asked to think first, then talk in a pair about their ideas and only then share with the whole class.

Now Try This

In a lesson you are teaching or observing, audio record (check that you will have permission to do this first) the talk of a small group working on a task. Your presence as a teacher can alter the nature, quality and quantity of talk considerably so it is important to audio record if you can. Begin by noting which pupils do the talking. Does one pupil dominate the talk and another one remains silent, or does each of the pupils contribute significantly? Are the pupils talking collaboratively or cooperatively? In other words, are they building on each other's ideas and clearly listening to each other, or is the talk focused on completing the task, possibly sounding like discrete conversations overlapping?

PUPILS' ROLES IN DISCUSSION

In many classes pupils have few opportunities to discuss mathematics. Even when they are used to working in small groups, as has been discussed in Chapter 6, there is often cooperation rather than collaboration between the pupils. In whole-class interactions, the dialogue is often between the teacher and a pupil, and is rarely between pupil and pupil. Pupils can build on one another's responses and can direct their questions towards other pupils. Supporting collaborative working in whole-class situations takes some skill but is worth the effort. If you observe many lessons, you will probably notice that the eyes of the pupils are usually focused on the teacher and that questions are rarely asked by pupils. It does not have to be like this.

One way to support pupils in listening to their peers' contributions and building on them is to model the type of responses you want them to give. You could:

- contrast responses from different pupils;
- summarise or synthesise the pupils' ideas;
- elaborate or explain individual pupil's contributions and then ask them to agree with your elaboration or explanation, for example 'Peter said . . . but Kate argued that . . .'; 'so . . ., is that what you mean?'

Over time your pupils will develop the skill to use these ways of responding independently, without the discussion needing to be managed by the teacher. In order for this to happen they must become used to thinking about others' responses and contributing their own ideas. A step on the way to this is to invite the pupils to explicitly discuss a contribution that a particular pupil has made. You might use prompts such as 'Does anyone want to say that differently?', 'Can anyone summarise what Robert and Clare have said?', 'Does anyone want to ask Andrea a question?' or 'How does your idea differ from Ian's?'

Now Try This

Use some of the prompts above or similar ones in your own teaching. Note down the responses the pupils make to each of them. To what extent do you feel the pupils were listening to each other and building upon each other's responses?

Setting out 'ground rules' such as were discussed in Chapter 6 can help make the discussion proceed more smoothly. For example, Mercer established 'talking rules' when working with primary and lower secondary age pupils: 'we share our ideas and listen to each other, we talk one at a time, we respect each other's opinions, we give reasons to explain our ideas, if we disagree we ask "why", we try to agree at the end' (Mercer 2000, pp. 161–2).

SUPPORTING AND DEVELOPING DISCUSSION

There are many approaches that can create an environment in which pupils are happy to share, discuss and debate ideas. One of the key features of such an environment is that you show the pupils that you are genuinely listening to their contributions. Questioning often involves a teacher asking a question to which they already know the answer, and this can result in the teacher hearing the answer they were expecting and then moving on. Asking a question that you genuinely want to know the answer to and then listening carefully to what your pupils have to say will indicate more than any other action the type of environment that you want to have in your classroom. Showing that you are both interested in and want to understand what they are saying helps to support the type of environment in which pupils will discuss mathematics.

One simple technique to show you are listening instead of evaluating a pupils' response is to just say 'mmm, hmm'. This shows the pupil that you have heard and understood them, but also invites them to continue and expand their response. If you do not understand what they are trying to say, you can ask them questions about their meaning, such as 'What do you mean by . . .?' or ask them to give an example. Leaving pauses between both your questions and a pupil's answer and the answer and your response also encourages pupils to expand, explain or correct their answers.

Now Try This

Next time you find yourself taking answers from your pupils, stop yourself from evaluating as right or wrong or even acknowledging answers with 'okay'. Instead, ask another pupil what they think about the answer that has been given, or whether they have anything to add to it. Asking questions in ways that everyone can answer (it is possible, but unlikely, that a pupil will answer 'I am not thinking'!) will encourage pupils to make these evaluations.

Another way to demonstrate that you are genuinely listening to the pupils' contributions is to attribute them to the pupil who gave them. For example, 'Nick said . . . and George added to this by . . .'. This helps to give pupils ownership of the mathematics under discussion whilst at the same time ensuring that all the pupils have heard what was said by Nick or George.

Another advantage to giving pupils ownership of the discussion is that they develop the skills of assessing the appropriateness of different contributions, rather than relying on the teacher to make these assessments.

Task

Observe another teacher who uses discussion a great deal in their own teaching (this may need to be a teacher from another curriculum area such as English or history). Consider what it is that this teacher does to create a safe environment for discussion and then to support pupils in taking part in whole-class discussions.

ALTERNATIVE FORMS OF COMMUNICATION

Communicating mathematically involves more than just being able to talk about mathematics. This chapter so far has focused on whole-class discussions and Chapter 6 has set out ideas for pupils to develop their discussion skills in small groups. The next part of this chapter focuses on other forms of communicating mathematically, such as presentations and writing.

PRESENTATION

Pupil presentations offer opportunities for pupils to describe the mathematics they have worked on or have engaged with. Resources will be needed but most importantly giving the pupils time to prepare will offer them the opportunity to question and consolidate their understanding. There is a great deal of variety in the nature of presentations that pupils can give. The most common form of pupil presentation in mathematics classroom is a reporting of progress and approach on an investigational task (see Chapter 8 for ideas about using investigations). This is most useful when the investigation is in progress and pupils present a variety of approaches. This allows a sharing of different ideas and approaches, but also offers an informal and useful assessment opportunity.

Another form of pupil presentation is to give a summary of an article they have read as homework. Reading a mathematical article once formed part of some A-level mathematics examinations and there are many sources of articles at this level (for example the MA publication *'Pig' and Other Tales* (French and Stripp 1997) or the Nrich website), but other sources could include popular mathematics books such as those by Ian Stewart, Rob Eastaway or Martin Gardner.

Other ideas for presentations could include a 'sales pitch' where students have to sell a mathematical object such as a cube or a rhombus. Similarly, pupils could act out a news bulletin where the mathematical object is wanted by police or introduce the object as a world famous host for today's show. There are also word games such as Fourbidden (ATM) (similar to Taboo™) where pupils have to describe a mathematical object without using a list of forbidden words. Pupils can take turns describing an object or you could run it as a competition of who can describe the most in a particular time period.

Now Try This

Choose a short article or book chapter about a mathematical idea. Ask your pupils to read it and then prepare a presentation about the mathematics described and/or to design some questions for other pupils to answer based on the text.

Another accessible source of writing that includes mathematics is a newspaper, which often includes articles or adverts that contain something mathematically interesting. Adverts and articles with percentages in are particularly useful, as are league tables, or anything with graphs. There are a variety of things that pupils can read and present: from the basic identification of the mathematical content, to a discussion of whether they think the data is being presented in a misleading way; this can also, in turn, lead into an interesting debate if there is a difference of opinion.

WRITING

Communicating mathematically includes writing mathematically. Pupils often find writing mathematics and writing about mathematics difficult. Most of the written mathematics that pupils experience involves copying down questions and completing answers in a set pattern. One method that you can use to support your pupils in writing mathematically is by asking them to design their own questions, perhaps for a future assessment. Another common strategy is to ask pupils to design a revision guide or a summary for other pupils on the topic you are currently studying. They could also construct a newspaper report which includes words and numbers and possibly charts and graphs. This would help remind the pupils that real-world mathematical writing is about communicating and uses words and numbers. It will be important to remind your pupils that simply downloading and printing pages from the internet is not what you are looking for. Limit the amount of writing and remind them that the purpose of the writing is to help them understand the mathematics they are to write about. Pupil journals are also increasingly being used as a way for pupils to keep their own records of what they are learning in mathematics.

Now Try This

In a revision lesson ask pupils to design their own revision guide, summary or even their own test. How easy do they find writing in this way? What assessment information about their understanding were you able to gain from this activity?

Pupils used to make a record of a mathematical investigation as part of the GCSE assessment, but now with no coursework element to the examination, pupils often do not experience the discipline of writing up an investigation or an extended piece of mathematics. One way to offer the opportunity to develop this skill is to give the role of recorder to a member of a small group who are working on an investigation. The need for writing is further reinforced if the pupils are asked to report back to the rest of the class using their record. Another way would be to structure writing time into the task itself. However, if pupils are unaccustomed to writing in this way, you will need to support the process initially with writing frames, or examples. Reading mathematics that is similar to that which you want your pupils to write in can also help them to develop the necessary skills.

Task

For an investigative task you have seen used or are planning to use, design a writing frame or model of the writing you consider would help your pupils to communicate their ideas.

This chapter has touched on a wide range of issues relating to communicating mathematically. Creating a classroom where pupils are comfortable and confident in communicating in a variety of ways is challenging and requires a lot of support and encouragement from you as a teacher. Not all of the strategies suggested will work first time or all of the time, but improving and supporting communication in your classroom will help pupils to think about and learn more mathematics and enjoy and succeed in the subject.

SUMMARY

In this chapter you were invited to think about how much your pupils communicate when learning mathematics and how to develop their communication and mathematical thinking and learning. The chapter explored:

- why increasing communication in mathematics can help pupils learn more;
- how whole-class discussions can be initiated;
- the pupils' role in whole-class discussions;
- creating an environment where discussions can be supported and developed;
- modelling ways of responding in discussions and setting out ground rules;
- using presentations to help your pupils learn effectively;
- using reading and writing in the classroom to bring real-world communications into the learning environment.

FURTHER READING

ATM (2004) *Thinkers*, Derby: Association of Teachers of Mathematics (ATM).

Henning, John E. (2008) *The Art of Discussion-Based Teaching: Opening Up Conversation in the Classroom*, New York and London: Routledge.

Lee, C. (2006) *Language for Learning Mathematics: Assessment for Learning in Practice*, Maidenhead, UK: Open University Press.

Chapter 8   Enquiry as a vehicle for teaching and learning mathematics

MIKE OLLERTON

Using investigative approaches in mathematics classrooms is, I believe, the most interesting and powerful way of enabling mathematical learning. This is because when students explore, try things out, play with ideas and seek solutions to puzzles and problems, they become more interested in mathematics and more mathematically capable.

There are many reasons for using investigative approaches as the main vehicle for both teaching and learning mathematics. These reasons include enabling:

- pupils to construct and develop knowledge beyond the ceiling of any syllabus;
- teachers to do less talking to a whole class and have more interactions with individuals or small groups of pupils;
- teachers to use a wider range of approaches with pupils who have diverse needs and different speeds and depths of learning potentials;
- pupils to become more active explorers of mathematics;
- pupils to develop, use and apply crucial mathematical thinking skills;
- pupils to engage first-hand with the interconnectivity of mathematical concepts.

I develop each of these issues presently.

The word 'investigations' has become synonymous with other phrases such as problem-solving, rich tasks, discovery learning and using and applying mathematics. The notion of learning mathematics through investigative approaches came to prominence in the Cockcroft Report published in 1982, possibly through the widely quoted paragraph 243. Cockcroft was closely followed in 1985 by a seminal publication, HMI's *Mathematics from 5 to 16*, where one of the ten aims for teaching mathematics reads 'Imagination, initiative and flexibility of mind in mathematics' (p. 4), thereby highlighting key learning qualities. In 1987 *Better Mathematics* asked the question 'What makes a rich mathematical activity?' (Ahmed 1987, p. 20). In 1989 the National Curriculum Council's *Mathematics: Non-Statutory Guidance* (NCC 1989) was published, which is another superb piece of work, setting out the bases of activities for teaching and learning mathematics, for example: 'Activities should be balanced between different modes of learning: doing, observing, talking and listening, discussing with other pupils, reflecting, drafting reading and writing, etc.' (section B7).

After a decade of deeply pedagogic publications I guess it was inevitable there would be a disaster waiting to befall the world of mathematics education. This arrived in the 1990s, when examination boards turned investigations into GCSE coursework which they assessed against detailed mark schemes, thus turning individual exploration into teacher-led prescription, which was subsequently labelled as cheating by successive governments. In the early years of the new millennium, coursework was to be abandoned in favour of 100 per cent terminal examinations. What started out, therefore, as a highly progressive opportunity to develop pupils' mathematical thinking became the Achilles' heel of progress in teaching and learning mathematics.

That is probably enough recent history for now and it is time to work on some mathematics! I invite you, therefore, to explore a task about consecutive sums, to experience for yourself the power and the potential of working investigatively. Basically a consecutive sum is the process of adding together sets of numbers which follow on, such as 6 + 7 or 1 + 2 + 3 + 4 or 12 + 13 + 14.

Choose any three consecutive numbers and add them together. Repeat this several times.

Keep a record of the numbers and the totals gained. Now choose four consecutive numbers and add these together; again repeat several times and keep a record of this information. Now consider the following two conjectures:

Conjecture 1: The total of any three consecutive numbers is divisible by 3 (with a remainder of 0).

Conjecture 2: The total of any four consecutive numbers is not divisible by 4 (with a remainder of 0).

Depending upon how much time you wish to devote to this problem, some further avenues could be:

- What kind of values can you gain when you total different quantities of consecutive numbers?
- Investigate those numbers, such as 15, which have several different consecutive sums.
- Investigate those numbers which have just one consecutive sum.
- Investigate those numbers that do not have any consecutive sums.
- Investigate those numbers whose consecutive sums always start at 1.
- Try to write an expression, in terms of n, to describe the sequence of totals formed by adding any four consecutive numbers.
- If you know the first number of a consecutive sequence and how many numbers there are in that sequence, how can you use this information to determine what the total will be?
- Consider summing other (linear) sequences, for example 5 + 7 + 9 + 11 + 13. Can you find a 'quick' way of arriving at the total without using addition?

Thus what started out as a simple piece of arithmetic has the potential to engage learners with a vast amount of mathematics about the properties of numbers as well as some 'simple' algebra. Indeed, the final two questions are clearly aimed at the summation of series, which is A-level content.

In considering tasks such as those noted above, and the claims I made earlier about working investigatively on mathematics, I offer the following analysis.

1. Pupils have a simple and, therefore, an accessible starting point task which, with perseverance, will take them into ever more complex areas of mathematics. Pupils will need to develop and use the generic personal quality of perseverance and the teacher can value pupils becoming ever more capable of working through 'stuckness' and developing other personal qualities such as independence and the confidence to support their peers. These qualities are discussed in many of the other chapters in this book (see, for example, Chapters 6 and 7) because they are important qualities for pupils to cultivate.

2. Since this problem is easy to pose, the teacher does not need to spend more than 5 or so minutes talking to the whole class before the pupils can make a start. Pupils do not need to listen to a lengthy whole-class teacher exposition; in any classroom where pupils have different concentration spans and different speeds and depths of cognition, this is an important consideration.

3. Instead of talking, the teacher can utilise other strategies such as 'paired-talk' and 'snowballing'. This means pupils do more of the talking, explaining, conjecturing, reasoning, justifying and proving. 'Thinking skills' must, educationally, be the most important set of skills any teacher of any subject would want pupils to cultivate. This issue is developed in greater depth in Chapter 6.

4. I am sure many of you, as children in school, were bored to death by the use of textbooks and the interminable exercises which the teacher marked with a tick or a cross in your exercise books. Textbooks rarely promote depth in mathematical thinking, although they can be used to do so (see Chapter 1). They are, at worst, a limiting resource which fragments the learning of mathematics into disparate skills and bits of knowledge.

Task

Here are another set of questions to ponder with regard to the summing consecutive numbers problem:

- How did you feel about working on the task?
- What different areas of mathematics did you find yourself applying your thinking to?
- How might you explain any of the results you arrived at?
- How might you prove any of the outcomes?
- What different processes did you engage with, for example what led you to choose your sets of numbers, how systematically did you work etc.?
- If requested (supposing this led to a qualification), would you be able to produce a 'write-up' to describe the work you did?

By seeking answers to these questions we inevitably engage with some of the key issues noted in the publications cited at the beginning of this chapter. The implications of using enquiry methods are to strengthen and deepen our understanding of the nature of mathematics (epistemology) as well as what it means to teach and to learn mathematics (pedagogy).

Offer the 'consecutive sums' task to a class you teach and consider as you plan for this lesson just how much talking you will need to do in order to enable the pupils to start working on the problem. You will also need to decide how you want to adapt the wording used above so the problem is clear for your class.

At the end of the lesson reflect on what happened, how pupils engaged or struggled with the task. Consider whether any of the five claims about working investigatively emerged in the lesson. Also consider whether the task has sufficient 'legs' for pupils to develop further their enquiry into a second or a third lesson.

Throughout the remainder of this chapter I present a range of puzzles, problems, investigations, and rich tasks (call them what you like!) in order to offer the reader, hopefully, a sense of awe and wonder with regard to seeing how complex mathematics can emerge from the most simple of starting points. I begin by offering ideas which can be taken into mathematics classrooms and without involving masses of planning. With each idea there is a task to consider.

Here, therefore, are some 'quickies':

a. **Joining triangles:** Give pupils, perhaps working in pairs, three cardboard triangles cut from the diagram shown in Figure 8.1.

The problem is to find all possible shapes using either two or three of the triangles and the condition that the triangles can only be joined by a common edge length.

Figure 8.1 Joining triangles

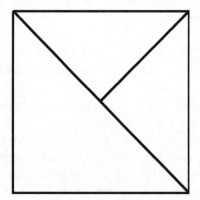

How will you know that you have found all possible shapes?

Can you prove you have found them all?

What other mathematical ideas might this idea lead towards?

b. **Blobs and joins:** With 5 blobs in a straight line a minimum of 4 joins (join: a line joining two blobs) can be created.

In this exploration a 'blob' represents a point. If blobs are arranged as in the diagram shown in Figure 8.2, 7 joins are made (I have made the blobs bigger in order to make the diagram easier to see).

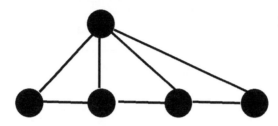

Figure 8.2
Blobs and joins

Conditions: joins must be straight lines though they do not need to be of the same length and lines can cross.

Task

Finding the minimum number of joins produces a simple linear sequence; finding the maximum number of joins produces a quadratic sequence. However, exploring the second highest number of joins creates a different challenge; perhaps you may like to take the challenge.

---

c. **A number puzzle**
   - Write down any three different digits.
   - Make all the possible 2-digit numbers using combinations of these three digits (you should be able to find six of these 2-digit numbers).
   - Add these six 2-digit numbers together.
   - Divide your answer by 22. (One way to do this is to divide your total by 2 then divide this answer by 11.)
   - Write down your answer.

Now return to the original three digits you wrote down at the start, add these three digits together. What do you notice? Why does it happen?

Task

Consider how you might extend this task for older or for higher achieving students.

The following three tasks will take more planning and a little more time to set up with a class.

d. **Fibonacci number cells:** This idea is aimed, eventually, at developing pupils' symbolic manipulating skills. Ask your pupils to work in pairs, each individual produces an agreed number of 5-cell Fibonacci-type sequences; that is, they choose *any* pair of starting numbers then calculate the next three.

Having done this they give their partner the first and the last value for each set of numbers; pupils then have to try to calculate each others' missing values.

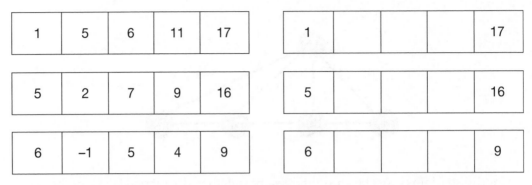

Figure 8.3 Five-cell Fibonacci-type sequences

In Figure 8.3, the final 5-cell sequence involves using directed numbers. This can be suggested as a further extension task, as could the use of fractions. A development is to suggest pupils try to construct a formula to describe how **f** (the first) and **l** (the last) numbers in each 5-cell, can be manipulated in order to find **m** (the middle) number.

Task

Explore formulae for finding the middle values of 7-, 9-, and 11-cell problems given the first and the last values.

---

e. **Exploring addition**

You have the digits $\boxed{1}$ $\boxed{2}$ $\boxed{3}$ and $\boxed{4}$ together with

one addition sign $\boxed{+}$ and the equals sign $\boxed{=}$

The idea is to arrange the cards to make different totals when you add two 2-digit numbers together. For instance, this total is 55:

$$\boxed{3}\ \boxed{1}\ \boxed{+}\ \boxed{2}\ \boxed{4}\ \boxed{=}$$

- How many different totals can be made?
- How do you know you have found them all?
- What are the minimum and maximum totals?
- Arrange your totals from smallest to largest and calculate the difference between successive pairs.
- What do you notice about the differences?

- Suppose you started with four other consecutive digits, what do you notice about the totals this time?
- Find maximum and minimum values for n, n + 1, n + 2, n + 3.

Task

Try to prove why the differences are always 9. What happens if you choose any four starting numbers? How might you algerbrise this latter situation?

f. Stars and statistics

The following idea was first introduced to me, as a young teacher, in 1975 by my head of department, Eric Love. I mention Eric because his ideas about the use of investigative approaches to teaching and learning mathematics were several decades ahead of the time. This idea also appears in the Association of Teachers of Mathematics (ATM) publication *Learning and Teaching Mathematics Without a Textbook* (Ollerton 2002, pp. 9–10).

Quite simply, 'all' one has to do is to project the image shown in Figure 8.4 on a screen for no more than 10 seconds (from the moment when you have drawn the attention of the class to it).

Next, give each pupil a sticky note and ask them to (a) write their initials on it and (b) 'secretly' write down their estimate of how many stars they saw. The idea behind asking them to write down their estimate, instead of asking them to call out answers, is so pupils are not influenced by the first couple of answers to be offered. Collect the sticky notes in and record their initials and their estimates on the board/screen. A further reason for asking them to write their initials is so you can return their sticky notes to them later in the lesson or at the beginning of the following lesson in order for students to write a second estimate.

As you are writing initials and estimates on the board, perhaps using a spreadsheet, pupils can copy this information into their exercise books. Once all the information has been recorded, ask the question: 'How can we use this information to arrive at an "agreed" class answer?' Note, I purposefully do not use the word 'average' because on the dozens of occasions I have used this idea with Year 7 (and younger pupils), all the different averages emerge. There is a crucially important issue here, which is that I don't need to teach Year 7s what the mode, median and mean are because some of them already know. Furthermore, those that know can explain to those who don't, or those who have forgotten. As such, this becomes a far more powerful 'lesson' for everyone involved.

Sometimes, somebody asks whether calculating the middle value between the smallest and the largest estimates would be useful and, interestingly enough, it is surprising just how accurate this can be. If such a suggestion is not made, then offer it and suggest the description as a 'quick average'.

Task

Think about all the different ways this information can be analysed and displayed and therefore what kind of activities students could be asked to carry out.

Figure 8.4 Stars and statistics

At the beginning of the following lesson I return the sticky notes, display the image a second time, again for just a few seconds, and ask them to write a second estimate. Again I collect these in and record them on the board/screen. This second set of data is likely to have a reduced range and there will now be many opportunities to compare the two data sets graphically and in terms of percentage differences between each pair of estimates, providing a useful in-context opportunity for pupils to engage with the process of calculating percentage differences, though perhaps not necessarily with a Year 7 class.

Now Try This

Take the 'stars and statistics' idea into two classrooms, for example a Year 7 class and a Year 10 class. Reflect on the differences in the way each class engaged with the task.

The final group of tasks is likely to benefit pupils' learning if they have access to certain types of practical equipment which provide students with opportunities to 'play around' with ideas.

THE SQUARE 9-PIN GEOBOARD

This piece of equipment is one through which vast swathes of the mathematics curriculum can be accessed and I invite you to consider the following task:

Task

How many 'different' (non-congruent) triangles can be made on a square 9-pin geoboard?

You might find the grids on the following page useful, but it also possible to use geoboards on an interactive whiteboard, on computer screens or tablets and your pupils can even display and interact with them on their phones (see Chapters 3 and 4).

Once you think you have found all possible different triangles, consider the following questions:

- Can you prove you have found them all?
- How might you describe the perimeters of each triangle?
- If the area of the whole grid is 4 square units, what are the areas of each triangle?
- Suppose we allow triangles which are congruent but not identical, how many are there now?
- Why is it not possible to form an equilateral triangle?
- What are the sizes of the angles of each triangle?

Of course, once all triangles on a square 9-dot grid have been explored, an obvious extension task could be to consider how many new triangles can be made

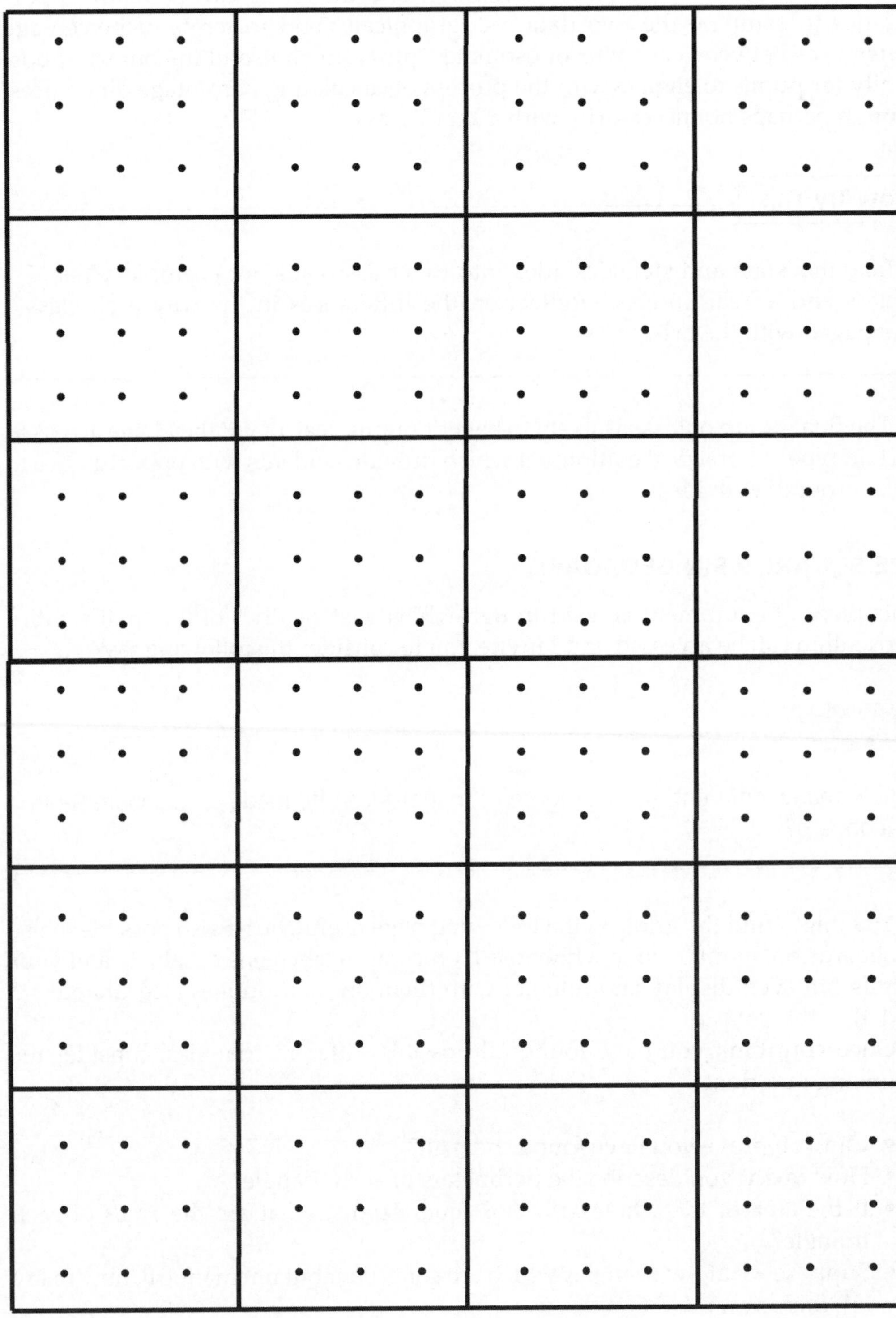

Figure 8.5 Square 9-pin geoboards

on a 16-dot grid. Again, all the earlier questions arising from triangles on a 9-dot grid can be asked of the 16-dot grid situation.

Calculating perimeters might be done algebraically by defining different lengths which can be made on the grid. Perimeters could also be defined using surds, thus the triangle below will have a perimeter of $1 + \sqrt{2} + \sqrt{5}$. For this, students will need to use their knowledge of Pythagoras' theorem.

Calculating the angles of the triangle shown in Figure 8.6 means pupils need to use and apply their trigonometric knowledge.

Whilst I refer to pupils using their knowledge of Pythagoras' theorem and trigonometry to develop a task, it is perfectly feasible to find investigative approaches to teaching these concepts and indeed any other concept. For example, investigative approaches to teaching trigonometry are described in *Inclusive Mathematics 11–18* (Ollerton and Watson 2001, pp. 113–20). The challenge is to find starting points from which pupils can construct knowledge and make sense of concepts. There are many publications within the domain of mathematics education which can be useful, such as those produced by the Association of Teachers of Mathematics and the Mathematical Association.

An important issue emerges here. Calculating perimeters using surds and angles using trigonometry means pupils can practise and consolidate existing knowledge. Thus the use of an investigative approach enables pupils to use and apply existing knowledge or recognise that they need to revisit certain skills which they do not have an 'at-homeness' (Cockcroft 1982, para 39) with. When such practice and consolidation opportunities arise, then we can replace the textbook; the ultimate challenge is to find a range of problems so the textbook can be dispensed with altogether!

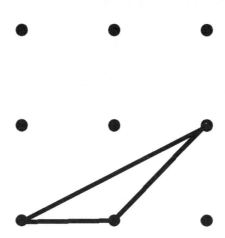

Figure 8.6 A triangle on a 9-pin geoboard

Task

The ideas above emerged essentially from a 'how many?' type problem. Try to construct other 'how many?' problems based on a 9-dot grid.

Task

Below are a few suggestions but no peeping until you have produced a list of your own!

Here are some of my favourite 'how many'-type problems:

- How many quadrilaterals?
- How many different angles?
- How many different straight lines in terms of y = mx + c (and x = c)?
- How many different crossing points are there formed by pairs of straight lines?
- How many vectors?
- How many different lengths of vectors?

Of course, each of these problems can be extended to a 16-dot grid and, indeed, the vectors problem could be extended to three-dimensional 8 or 27 dot grids – now there's a challenge which would rattle the brains of AS-level pupils.

There are still more problems that can be posed based upon the maximum perimeters of triangles on different sizes of grids and this can lead to an interesting generality (or two!).

Before leaving the subject of square dotty grids, here is one of my favourite problems, which is to calculate the area of overlap in the diagram shown in Figure 8.7. This is another splendid brain-scrambler that can be solved in different ways.

ASSESSING PUPILS' INVESTIGATIVE WORK

Assessing mathematical processes together with mathematical content knowledge is inevitably a complex issue. This is because, traditionally, mathematical content knowledge has been assessed in isolation through timed, written tests. However, key mathematical processes (such as simplifying a task, working systematically, pattern spotting, analysing data, seeking connections, interpreting data, writing conjectures, checking, proving, etc.) cannot be assessed using the same mechanism. Neither can broader, functional skills such as communication or the use of ICT be

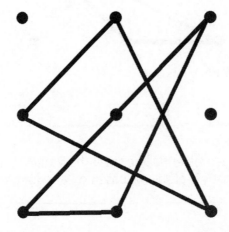

Figure 8.7 Calculate the overlap

assessed using a standard written test. A narrow mark-scheme type of approach constrains the breadth of mathematical thinking that is assessed and thus restricts investigative approaches.

Assessment should enable both you and your pupils to know that they are making progress and if there are any difficulties in particular areas. Thus any criteria used for assessment must be broad and flexible enough to recognise progress in the mathematical ideas used and the thinking being done. The intention of the APP materials (DCSF 2008) was that investigative skills would be assessed against the criteria set out in the section of the criteria entitled 'Using and Applying Mathematics'. Some schools do use these materials successfully but others have decided that their complexity is overwhelming. They are likely to be superseded in the near future in England.

My colleague Daniela Vasile, of the South Island School, Hong Kong, uses just four criteria to assess students' work. Informal assessment information on each of these criteria is gathered over the course of 'units' of work, each of which lasts three to four weeks. The criteria are:

1. **Communication**

   In reports, whether oral or written, you will show:
   a. the correct use of mathematical terminology, clarity and fluency of language, including the effective use of diagrams, table symbols and/or graphs;
   b. work that is structured in a way that is easy to follow and shows personal reflection.

2. **Structure of the mathematical content**

   Your work will show:
   a. ideas presented in a logical, systematic way enabling students to seek patterns and form conjectures;
   b. data are generated/gathered and organised, leading to generalities being formed;
   c. information analysed and conclusions made, possibly leading to proof.

3. **Concept development and accuracy**

   Your work will show:
   a. a clarity of understanding of mathematical concepts;
   b. correct working, appropriately accurate, and self-checked.

4. **What makes a mathematical investigation worthwhile**

   In the types of questions you ask and the interesting or unexpected ideas you devise whilst working on a project, you will show
   a. creativity in your work;
   b. engagement with a task or problem, positive attitudes and enthusiasm.

The use of investigative approaches in the mathematics classroom, together with the types of approaches discussed in Chapters 6 and 7 makes for a healthy learning environment. Pupils become ever more independent thinkers and communicators of mathematics, go ever deeper into their understanding of 'new' concepts and use and apply existing ones in purposeful more interesting and engaging ways.

SUMMARY

In this chapter you were invited to think about using enquiry methods as part of teaching and learning mathematics. The discussion included:

- how investigative approaches can be used to engage and motivate pupils;
- particular reasons for using an investigative approach;
- the importance of an accessible start to the task and how tasks can be extended;
- the role of the teacher when working in this way;
- how investigations can enable pupils to work more independently and develop skills of perseverance and supporting others;
- how short enquiries can be introduced in lessons and some ideas that can be used;
- the use of investigations and the kinds of mathematics that can emerge after a relatively simple start;
- how progress in investigative or process based skills can be assessed.

FURTHER READING

Foster, C. (2010) *Resources for Teaching Mathematics*, London: Continuum.

Gardner, M. (2006) *Aha! A Two Volume Collection: Aha! Gotcha, Aha! Insight*, Washington DC: The Mathematical Association of America.

Martin, C. (2011) *Big Ideas*, Derby: Association of Teachers of Mathematics.

Chapter 9   Taking mathematics outside

ROBERT WARD-PENNY

This chapter will introduce you to a range of ideas and activities which have one key feature in common – they all require you to step outside of the mathematics classroom. There are a number of potential benefits to teaching and learning mathematics 'outside': it can give pupils a chance to engage with concepts in an active, physical way; it can give rise to memorable and unusual experiences; and it can help demonstrate to your pupils that mathematics is something that is all around them, everyday and everywhere.

PLANNING TO GO OUTSIDE

Before taking pupils outside of the classroom, it is important to think about how you are going to manage both the pupils' behaviour and their learning. It is critical to select and structure activities in a way that is appropriate for each individual group. This is a matter for your own professional judgement, but you may find the following tips useful:

- Try to give the pupils clear instructions *before* leaving the classroom. It is generally harder to gain and hold pupils' attention once they are outside.
- Set clear boundaries. Where should the pupils assemble, and how far can they go in each direction? How long will they have before they are to report back to you, or return to the classroom?
- If you have a teaching assistant or mentor available to support you, try to brief them beforehand and direct their time and attention. (If you are on teaching practice, it is also sensible to check any plans with your school-based mentor first to make sure you are working within school guidelines.)
- Finally, establish some ground rules with the pupils about going outside during your lesson. What do you expect? Is there anything that would cause you to stop the activity short and return inside?

> **Task**
>
> Write down one or two basic 'ground rules' which you would share with your pupils before going outside.

MAKING THE MOST OF THE SPACE AVAILABLE

Outside areas usually offer the pupils more space to move around in, and you can sometimes direct them to 'become', or enact, mathematical ideas. One good example is the topic of loci. If you 'fix' one pupil and ask the other pupils to stand exactly three metres away from them, they have discovered for themselves the locus of points equidistant from a fixed point. Similarly, if you 'fix' two pupils and ask the remaining pupils to stand equidistant from them both, they should together form a perpendicular bisector. These experiences can then be discussed and built upon in the classroom. This approach works well in a number of areas of the curriculum, for example, A-level mechanics frequently lends itself to experiments and demonstrations.

Task

How might you direct a class of Year 10 pupils so that they 'construct' an angle bisector in this manner?

You might start to investigate a piece of mathematics outside. One common mathematics investigation involves 12 people standing in a circle. If they pass the ball around the circle in jumps of n, which values of n will result in everyone having the ball at some point? What if we started with a different number of people? Introducing this investigation outside allows pupils to clearly visualise what is going on, as well as to make and test initial hypotheses.

Being outside also offers a lot of opportunities to collect data. For instance, you might get the pupils to measure their heart rates, do laps of the playground for 3 minutes and then measure their heart rates again. This type of activity could stimulate a lesson involving back-to-back stem-and-leaf plots.

Different spaces offer different opportunities. If you have access to a dance hall with mirrors, how might you use it to inspire the pupils to explore reflection? If your grounds have particularly tall trees, could the pupils use clinometers during a trigonometry lesson to calculate their height? If the school playground has interesting features, could you send the pupils out to create a scale plan? With a larger playground, you might even allocate separate sections of the playground to groups of pupils, and then see if their plans can be successfully combined at the end of the lesson.

Now Try This

Choose or adapt one of the ideas in this section to use as part of a lesson. Whilst you are teaching the lesson, watch the pupils to see how going outside has impacted upon their attitudes and their mathematical learning.

EVERYONE LIKES A TREASURE HUNT

The next part of this chapter will suggest three different ways in which you can use outdoor space to enhance and structure learning in mathematics lessons. The first of these is perhaps the easiest to organise. Instead of setting your class a set of questions from a worksheet or textbook, you might print out the questions in a large font, and then place them around a bounded outdoor space, such as a playground. Pupils have to work their way around the playground in pairs, aiming to present you with a correct set of answers in the time allowed. You can use this idea inside – I have managed to conduct a 'PythagoRace' in my classroom, through a judicious use of cupboard doors – but setting it up outside can add a little more variety to the pupils' learning experience.

A second framing device is an 'algebra run'. Begin by taking some photos of places where numbers occur around the outside of your school – again, it is safest and easiest to make sure these fall within a bounded, easily described area such as a playground. Next, cover over one digit from each photo, replacing them with letters. The pupils are presented with a sheet of doctored photos and algebraic expressions. To complete the task they need to locate the missing numbers and substitute them correctly; perhaps this could help them uncover a message, or deduce a code which unlocks a padlock.

Hidden questions and 'algebra runs' can both be quite motivating, but it is good practice to plan ahead and include opportunities for learning which move beyond simply practising a technique. For instance, the pupils could work in teams to generate and hide questions for each other, or to take photos and construct their own algebra run. Photographic contexts can also act as starting points for interesting discussions: do your pupils understand what the numbers on a yellow 'H' fire hydrant marker represent? Given that the speed limit sign in Figure 9.1a is 10 miles per hour, why is it straightforward to evaluate an expression such as $A(C^3 + 1)$? What is the most challenging expression the pupils can come up with, using the letter values provided?

Task

Take a look around from where you are sitting at the moment. How many places can you spot where numbers are visible?

A third, slightly more ambitious option is to set up a mathematics treasure hunt, where each clue requires the pupils to apply some mathematics. You might construct it so that each question leads the next question, so that the questions lead to letters which have to be unscrambled to form a mathematical word, or you might

Figures 9.1a and 9.1b Missing digits for an algebra run

choose another method entirely – this will depend on your group, and the amount of time and space you have available. Similarly, there are hundreds of ways to construct clues. Here are a few ideas to start you off:

- Give the pupils a map of the school playground with a coordinate grid imposed over the top, and a series of coordinates.
- Find an aerial map of the school and mark on two landmarks, A and B. Explain to the pupils that the next clue lies at a point C, where the distances from A to C and B to C are in the ratio 1:2.
- Turn one of the clues into cipher text, either using a straightforward method such as a Caesar square or a more complicated one, perhaps using arithmetic modulo 26.

Again, it is valuable to think ahead to opportunities for developing the pupils' mathematical thinking. How do the coordinate map clues in the first suggestion above relate to GPS coordinates? Why there are two possible solutions to the second question and what would happen to each of the points if we altered the ratio to 1:3, 1:4, or 1:1000?

Now Try This

If it is appropriate for one of your classes, adapt and use one of the following ideas: hiding questions to find and complete; an 'algebra run'; a mathematics treasure hunt. Take a couple of minutes afterwards to discuss the activity with the pupils – did they enjoy it, and do they feel that it supported their learning?

MATHS TRAILS

Mathematics has been described as a 'chameleon discipline'; although it can be found almost anywhere, it often fades away against the background of a particular situation. One of the tasks of the mathematics teacher is therefore to encourage pupils to see the mathematics that surrounds them, and to make connections between classroom-based exercises and real-life contexts. This is also the goal of a maths trail.

A maths trail is a path or loop which contains a number of waypoints where the pupils have to do some mathematics. This is important. Unlike the algebra run described above, at each waypoint the pupils do not simply spot a number but actively engage with some of the mathematics that can be found there.

As a common, but extremely dull example, consider a standard brick wall. Even here there is a lot of potential for questions which develop mathematical thinking at a number of levels:

- What shape are the bricks?
- As the bricks fill up space in a regular pattern without gaps, we can say that they *tessellate*. Name two other tessellating 3-D shapes that could also be used for bricks. Why do you think builders use this shape instead of your suggestions?
- Measure the height of one of the bricks to the nearest centimetre. How many bricks high is the school at this point? Use your measurement to estimate the height of the school – how accurate do you think your answer is? Why?

You will probably be able to think of some other questions, and which questions are appropriate will of course depend on the pupils undertaking the maths trail. However, this very simple example has hopefully demonstrated that even the least inspiring situation can give rise to some genuine mathematical challenges. How many more can you generate by looking at more interesting features, such as the areas of tennis courts, the seating capacity of the canteen, or the gradients of different steps and ramps in your school grounds? A basic example of a maths trail is provided in Figure 9.2. Here the teacher has combined the clues with a map to make the route very clear to their pupils.

Now Try This

Take some time to walk around your school site. Note down four or five places which you think could give rise to some mathematics. If you feel sufficiently confident, develop these notes into a maths trail and try it out with one of your classes.

Using the school site is only one way in which you might use a maths trail with your classes. With the support of your school, you might choose to develop a maths trail off site, so that pupils can walk around a local park or museum and extract mathematics from a slightly more unfamiliar setting. Alternatively, you might ask the pupils to develop their own maths trails in groups, then swap over and test out another group's route and questions. However you choose to adapt the idea, the experience of a maths trail will support the pupils in identifying some of the mathematics that lies hidden in the world around them.

NOTICING MATHEMATICS

Although going outside offers a number of particular advantages, it is not always practical or optimal to take classes outside. The last part of this chapter will therefore suggest some classroom-based ways to encourage pupils to notice mathematics in the world around them.

A good way to begin is to consider what mathematics might be local to you. This might be quite subtle – for instance, perhaps there is a nearby garage which the pupils pass on the way to school, or even which you can see from your window. Noting down the prices of diesel and unleaded petrol once a week on a spreadsheet can give rise to a real-life line graph, as well as discussions about seasonal trends, moving averages and extrapolation. A similar activity could involve regularly recording the outside temperature.

A more pronounced approach is to consider the mathematics involved in any landmarks or geographical features local to your school. For instance, consider the London Eye (Figure 9.3). This could easily serve as a starting point for questions about circumference, angles, speed and capacity.

1) Outside Room M2

Before you begin each of you must make an estimate of the number of steps you think you will take on the maths trail. Calculate the mean of your estimates. Use the pedometer as you go around, and at the end of the trail see who was closest.

2) Outdoor Amphitheatre

What is the diameter of the small paved circle? What is the diameter of the large paved circle? How many times bigger is the diameter of the large circle? How many times bigger is the area of the large circle?

3) Canteen

The canteen is always nearly full at lunch. Using the fact that there are 1200 pupils in the school, estimate the percentage of pupils who use the canteen.

4) Athletics Track

Work out the area enclosed by the innermost running track. Why are the starts of the lanes staggered?

5) School Logo on the Side of the Maths Block

Describe as fully as you can all of the symmetries in the school logo. Why do you think logos often include symmetry in their design?

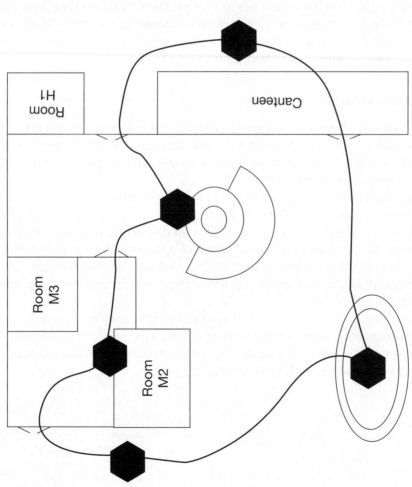

Figure 9.2 An example of a maths trail

Figure 9.3 What mathematics is there in the London Eye?

Task

Write down three landmarks or geographical features that are local to your area. Select one, and devise at least three related mathematical questions. Can you develop this into a starter activity of some kind?

One final idea is to bring real-life photos into the classroom and use them as starting points for mathematical activity and discussion. You can find many suitable photos online – Chapter 3 talks about how you might use Google Earth to do this – but you might like to take some photos of your own, or even share one or two appropriate holiday snaps with your pupils!

The photo in Figure 9.4 is offered here as an example. This image could lead to a discussion about symmetry, or introduce a lesson on quadratic graphs. What would happen if we changed the water pressure? What would happen if we changed the angle of the spouts? Some ICT programmes now allow you to import photos and draw graphs over the top, so a photo like this could support a curve-fitting activity. Yet again, it is worth contemplating whether you might open this activity out to the pupils. Could you ask them to find or take a 'maths photo' which they have to present to the class with a brief explanation of the mathematics involved?

Figure 9.4 What mathematics is there in this picture?

CONCLUSION

Taking mathematics outside of the classroom can help to motivate learners and to emphasise the relevance and utility of mathematics. It can lead to authentic cross-curricular contexts, add variety to your teaching, and bring about memorable experiences. Although you will need to give proper thought to issues of behaviour management, permission, and health and safety, teaching practice is a great time to try out some of the ideas discussed above for yourself, and to encourage your pupils to spot a little of the mathematics that surrounds them every day.

SUMMARY

In this chapter you were invited to think about enabling your pupils to learn mathematics using the real world outside the classroom and a number of elements that can be used were discussed including:

- planning to go outside the classroom and what you must consider before you do;
- the kinds of activities that the pupils might learn from using an outside space;
- setting up a treasure hunt type activity to support mathematical learning;
- how to set up a maths trail and how it can be used to show your pupils that mathematical ideas occur everywhere;
- how noticing mathematical situations around you can encourage your pupils to spot the mathematics around them.

Chapter 10 Active and creative mathematics

NICK MCIVOR

One of the main ideas underpinning this chapter is that mathematics itself is a game. As in all games there is a set of agreed rules, such as 1 + 1 = 2 and that division is the inverse of multiplication; unlike most games, however, the objectives can seem rather obscure. Teachers sometimes try to rationalise mundane topics like percentages by suggesting that they are preparing their pupils for life in the outside world. Anyone who has ever tried this in a classroom will be aware of how badly this can backfire. Most shops do not expect customers to work out their own discounts and most workplaces do not require staff to calculate their own tax. The last refuge for a desperate teacher in search of a purpose is the 'it's in the GCSE' ploy. Although this can be effective in the short term it is ultimately self-defeating as it simply reinforces the suspicion among many pupils that the purpose of maths is to provide content for examinations. However, there is another, simpler purpose for all games: the participants should have fun playing them. The games described below have proved themselves in a range of different classroom settings to be engaging and enjoyable for learners.

WHOLE-CLASS 'GENERIC' GAMES

These are teacher-led activities that can be adapted to cover a wide range of topics, but are probably most useful for reinforcing number skills.

Kung fu master

The teacher selects a topic that the class needs to practise, for instance, finding fractions of numbers. Two pupils *of comparable skill in this topic* are invited to stand up in their places and face each other across the classroom; they are now in the 'dojo' or martial arts training ground and show respect for each other through a shallow bow. The teacher or 'sensei' now calls out a question such as '¾ of 24' and each competitor has to call out the answer as quickly as possible. The first correct answer wins. The loser sits and another pupil stands to challenge the winner or 'kung fu master'. When a pupil has won three consecutive bouts (surprisingly difficult if the teacher chooses pairings wisely) s/he is deemed to have ascended to the next level of martial arts mastery and is rewarded with a certificate. Martial arts gradings can easily be found online and each teacher or department can settle on their own ranking system, the one I use is: white belt, green belt, brown belt and then black belt.

A practised teacher can get through 10 to 15 bouts in 5 minutes, so two 5-minute sessions can allow an entire class to participate. Note that although any topic can be used, the questions must be simple enough to be calculated mentally. It is important to take a pupil's first answer or a succession of loud guesses from one competitor will prevent a quieter pupil from joining in. If a pupil's first answer is wrong, the other player has between 5 and 10 seconds to come up with a correct answer – I usually count back from five using my fingers – if neither player answers correctly two new pupils play.

> ### Task
>
> Think of a number-based lesson you have seen or taught recently. How could you have used the above activity as a mini-plenary to assess the learning that had taken place?

Team challenge

This requires some advance preparation of materials and the class needs to be grouped in threes or fours (or occasionally fives) at separate team tables. The original idea was inspired by a textbook which had sets of 12 questions arranged on 'cards' across double-page sections. Each double-page spread dealt with one topic, usually a straightforward arithmetic task such as addition or subtraction, but it is perfectly possible to use this approach for basic algebra. Suppose your class is arranged in seven groups of three or four, each group is given a large sheet of questions arranged in sets of 12. The teacher then issues the instruction 'Card Six' and each group has to finish all the questions on that card *with each pupil completing 3 questions in their own book*. This means a group of three pupils would only have to complete 9 questions in total. Any pupil who finishes early can help other team members *but must not write in anyone else's book*. This forces everyone to take an active part in the exercise. If you have groups of five, use only 10 questions and everybody has to complete 2 of them.

When the first team finishes all their questions everybody stops. The team who finished first gets a bonus point (or two) and answers are given. The teacher deducts a point for each wrong answer, and one for each calculation not completed. Each team gets a score out of 12 and the next round begins. This game has the advantage of allowing slightly more complicated, written questions than the other two games in this section.

Baseball

This works best with smaller groups (below 20 pupils) otherwise it can take too long for everyone to get a turn. If you have a teaching assistant and another space then two games can be played simultaneously. It is far easier to play with an interactive whiteboard which allows names to be dragged around the screen. Draw a baseball diamond on the board as shown below and a list of names for each team. Decide which team is 'pitching' (bowling) and which team is 'hitting' (batting), then drag the pitcher's name to the mound and the hitter's name to the plate (use sticky notes and a flip chart if an interactive whiteboard is not available.)

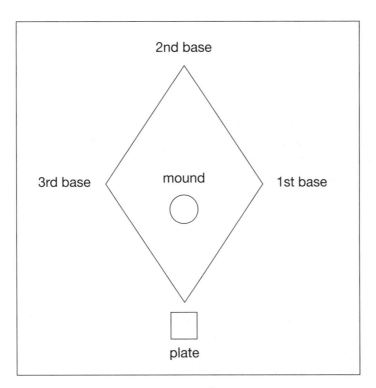

Figure 10.1 Baseball diamond

The player who is pitching asks a question such as -3 + -4.

The hitter has five seconds to answer the question.

If the hitter is correct, their name is moved to first base and all the hitters currently on the field move on one more base.

If the hitter is incorrect, a member of the pitcher's team is chosen at random (it's often a good idea to pick the least attentive one) and has to answer the question correctly. A correct answer means the hitter is caught out, an incorrect answer means the catch has been fumbled and the hitter moves to first base anyway.

Whatever happens, a new pitcher and hitter are chosen each time. A run is scored each time a member of the hitting team returns to the home plate. Once three members of the hitting team are out, the whole team is out and a new innings begins.

In these three games the pupils are focused on winning for themselves or for their team. All of these activities have a competitive element, which can provide the imperative for the pupils to engage with the mathematical content. From the pupils' point of view, the mathematics is simply a means to an end and consequently they see a need to think and persevere. Care must be taken with the questions asked and the speed of answers required as many people have in the past become over anxious about mathematical thinking because they were 'put on the spot' in lessons. Try using pairs of pupils instead of individuals if your pupils need a confidence boost.

Now Try This

Plan a lesson which uses the team challenge or baseball as a main activity. During the lesson concentrate on keeping the pace fast enough to ensure that the activity feels like a game rather than an extended piece of teacher exposition.

MATHEMATICS LESSONS AS STORIES

Apart from the notion of mathematics as a game, the other main theme of this chapter is the idea that every lesson has a narrative. This is hardly controversial: the widely used starter–main–plenary structure is essentially a restating of 'beginning–middle–end'. What may sound slightly less conventional is the suggestion that information can, and sometimes should be withheld from learners until quite late in the lesson. Most surprising, perhaps, is the idea that under certain circumstances a teacher can keep pupils more engaged and help them learn more effectively by not telling them exactly what is going on.

To show how this can work in an actual lesson, it is probably most useful to consider another game.

Algebra four-in-a-row

This is one of the best ways of introducing algebra at Key Stage 3. It can be modified to guide pupils through constructing formulae and equations, solving equations and even drawing graphs, but the basic idea is simple: the class is divided into two or more groups (see Chapter 6 for a discussion of how to group pupils) and each team tries to make a straight line of four squares on a pre-drawn 100 grid. The lines can be horizontal, vertical or diagonal.

At the start of the lesson, pupils are given two learning intentions:

1. To learn a new game
2. ???????????????????

The second learning intention – algebra – is not mentioned at this point, so question marks are used. Tell the class to think about what the 'mystery objective' could be as the lesson continues.

Every pupil is asked to construct an input/output table in their books as follows:

input	output

Teams play by announcing numbers. If the red team plays '5' the teacher puts this number into a 'secret rule' (in this case add 6) and colours the *answer* on the hundred square red. Every pupil records the input and output then the next team plays. Here is an example of the first two turns:

input	output	
5	11	red
20	26	blue

Pretty soon, the pupils will start to figure out what the rule is. From the teacher's point of view this is the point of the game, but from the pupils' point of view the objective is to win by getting four of their colour squares in a row. Of course, knowing the rule gives either team a huge advantage so they are NOT allowed to shout it out. Instead they should simply write it at the foot of their table like this:

1	2	3	4	5	6	7	8	9	10
11	12	13	14	15	16	17	18	19	20
21	22	23	24	25	26	27	28	39	30
31	32	33	34	35	36	37	38	39	40
41	42	43	44	45	46	47	48	49	50
51	52	53	54	55	56	57	58	59	60
61	62	63	64	65	66	67	68	69	70
71	72	73	74	75	76	77	78	79	80
81	82	83	84	85	86	87	88	89	90
91	92	93	94	95	96	97	98	99	100

Figure 10.2 A hundred square

input	output	
5	11	red
20	26	blue

input + 6 → output

A bonus point can even be given to the first team who gets the rule correctly written in everybody's book *in their own writing*, as this forces team-members to explain the rule to each other.

A next step can be to change the headings at the top of table from input/output to x and y:

x	y	
5	11	red
20	26	blue

When this stage has been reached, the word 'algebra' may be introduced for the first time – or not as the teacher considers appropriate – now a bonus point can be given for the first team whose members correctly write the rule using letters:

$x + 6 = y$ or even $y = x + 6$

What drives this lesson for the pupils is the desire for their team to win a game. What makes it a useful teaching tool is that it creates a context in which algebra provides a convenient shorthand. In order for this lesson to have its full impact, it is imperative that the teacher does NOT mention algebra at the start of the lesson. Instead, the pupils 'discover' algebra as a useful tool which is very easy to understand. By introducing the subject as a practical tool for playing a game the question 'what is the point of algebra?' has been pre-empted.

In the final part of the lesson pupils can be asked to write their own version of 'the mystery objective' as a plenary-cum-assessment exercise. The way they articulate their responses can provide an interesting insight into their perception of algebra and its relationship to variables and rules.

> **Task**
>
> Think of how you could continue playing this game into a second or even third lesson and use it as a tool for introducing linear graphs in the first quadrant. Could you ask opposing teams to invent their own rules for the opposition to guess?

> **Now Try This**
>
> Use this game to introduce algebra to a group of younger pupils at your school. Try to devote as much time in the lesson as possible to actually playing the game and as little as possible to exposition. Introduce the word 'algebra' as late as you can.

The technique of holding back vital information can be is a useful way of introducing topics that pupils might perceive as difficult. In storytelling terms, this kind of lesson can be a journey into the unknown in which unfamiliar situations are resolved through new knowledge. What makes the above example particularly satisfying for the pupils is the realisation that they have been doing algebra all along without even realising – this makes them feel clever. Pupils will respect a teacher who makes them feel clever far more than one who convinces them that they are ignorant.

> **Task**
>
> Plan a lesson using the principle of keeping back information to introduce trigonometry. Perhaps you could use an investigative task such as calculating ratios of sides in similar triangles to help pupils 'discover' trigonometric ratios, or you could use some kind of practical measuring activity – such as measuring the height of a school building with an inclinometer – which becomes possible thanks to the tangent ratio. Can you think of a main objective to go alongside the 'mystery objective' for this lesson?

Of course the majority of lessons will not introduce a brand new topic, so the possibility of a 'big reveal' which offers algebra or trigonometry as the solution to a practical problem does not usually exist. For a lesson to maintain its narrative drive, however, it is important that the pupils have a sense that there is something new to be discovered. There is a truism in the theatre: when the audience knows every secret about every character they can go home; this can be translated into the classroom as when the learners know exactly what is going to happen at every subsequent moment they can stop paying attention. So how can a class be persuaded to remain engaged?

SURPRISES AND SPARE HOOKS

One of the over-arching themes throughout this book has been the importance of variety in planning the lessons for any group. Even within a strict starter–main–

plenary structure there are many different ways to approach each section. There are also different ways to navigate through each section which can create different experiences for learners.

FASCINATING RHYTHMS

Consider the situation when you are going to ask pupils to carry out a straight-forward calculation task such as finding fractions of whole numbers. The questions might be on the whiteboard or printed on a textbook page, but the format is unimportant, what matters is the rhythm you impose on the class as they work. For instance, you could set a time limit of five minutes for the class to complete as many questions as they can. This allows pupils time to settle into the task and gives you time to inspect some of their work and assess their level of understanding. It can create the sense of a 'breathing space' for teacher and learners, which can be very helpful. On the negative side, it can allow pupils the space to do little or nothing for several minutes before scrawling down some hasty answers in the last 30 seconds. An alternative approach would be to announce that answers will start appearing after one minute. When that minute is over, answers to the first five problems appear on the board, pupils check their answers then have to move on to the sixth, potentially more difficult problem. This brisk, high-energy approach can help to improve the work-rate among some pupils but can dishearten slower workers. A third, higher-risk approach would be to ask pupils to find pairs of questions with the same answer and allow them to find their own rhythm: some might start working methodically through every question; others might start by estimating before working out exact answers. Unfortunately, many are likely to spend a few seconds wondering what they are supposed to do before giving up completely.

   The key point about this way of thinking is that it asks you to reflect on the pace of work within each part of the lesson. Outside of an examination, very few classes will work flat out for an hour. Varying the pace is an important way to maintain the level of pupil engagement.

> **Task**
>
> Find a numerical starter activity that might be suitable for one of your current classes. Consider at least two different ways in which you could pace this activity. Which do you think would be more appropriate for your next lesson with them? Consider factors such as the time of day when the lesson is taking place and the point you have reached in the term.

SPARE HOOKS

Nearly every school lesson will have moments when the pupils seem to be losing focus. In a three-part lesson this is particularly common during the 'main' section: the topic has been introduced, pupils have begun work on the main task, but after starting quite enthusiastically the work-rate drops. As little as ten minutes may have passed – how can the class be re-engaged? One simple technique is to offer them a legitimate way of pausing for breath by offering a short, whole-class exposition on some aspect of the work being covered. This can be achieved in a number of ways:

- **Some mathematical trivia**: build up a repertoire of mathematical facts that can be thrown in to liven up a lesson. These can include bits of history such as 'algebra is an Arabic invention – the very word al jabr is Arabic in origin', or surprising applications of mathematics to everyday life: 'every time you buy anything online you rely on the amazing properties of prime numbers to keep your credit-card details secure.' (For more examples see widening your subject knowledge in Chapter 11.)
- **Clarifying a misconception**: as you have been monitoring pupils' work, you will nearly always find certain errors being repeated by several pupils. Use this as an opportunity for some whole-class teaching on that particular detail. Even if it directly benefits just two or three pupils, you can legitimately demand that all pupils either pay attention or continue working in silence. The exposition which should not be more than two minutes in length will therefore redirect those who are off-task without distracting the ones who may be working well.
- **Sharing good practice**: some pupils will have made better progress than others. Try sharing one of the pupil's ideas with the rest of the class, or better still, have the pupil concerned stand up and explain his or her approach. This is particularly appropriate when the task is an investigative one.

Task

Spend 15 minutes online and find out something you didn't already know about each of the four major topic areas in the maths curriculum – number, algebra, shape and data.

All of these interventions should end with a clear instruction for pupils to continue working for another fixed period. The effect of such a 'spare hook' should always be to bring the class back to your agenda, first by listening to you, then by getting on with what they were supposed to be doing in the first place. This approach tends to be more effective than yelling 'stop chatting and get on with your work', even if the subtext is precisely that.

Now Try This

The next time you are planning a lesson with an extended period devoted to independent pupil working, plan at least two possible interventions that might help to bring the class back on task when they start to drift. Aim to use just one of them during the lesson and if you have the confidence, decide which one to use during the lesson itself.

A SIDEWAYS JUMP

A famous TV comedy programme from the 1970s used the catchphrase 'and now for something completely different'. It disrupted the flow of what was going on and made the audience register that something new was about to happen. This section is the classroom version of that idea and returns to the idea of games, this time with a kinaesthetic dimension.

- **Sum throwing**: this can be adapted for any group who can be trusted not to throw things at each other. Take a mathematical operation – it can be as simple as adding 7 or as complicated as substituting a value into an algebraic expression – throw a bean bag to a random member of the class and say a number as you do so. Immediately after catching the bean-bag the pupil has to carry out the operation using the number they have been given. Repeat with another member of the class. If the classroom layout (and pupil behaviour) permits, getting the answer correct entitles that pupil to throw the bean-bag to somebody else, whilst choosing a new number.
- **Galloping gazintas**: this game is probably most useful for Year 7s and 8s. Every pupil writes a number between 2 and 9 on a mini-whiteboard. They stand with their numbers facing the teacher and begin galloping. If there is a classroom directly below it is probably best to do this by jogging the whiteboard up and down; if you are on the ground floor, pupils can jog on the spot. The teacher holds up a two-digit number, if a pupil's number 'goes into' the teacher's number, s/he remains standing, if their number does not 'go into' the teacher's number, the pupil sits. This can be played competitively as a kind of 'musical chairs' with pupils who make mistakes sitting out the next round.

There is of course a sense in which all mathematics lessons require learners to be active. Even the most mundane session is likely to involve activities such as 'working out solutions to problems using pen and paper' and the approaches suggested above simply lie on a different part of the activity spectrum. There is also a sense in which every lesson has the potential to be creative. This does not mean every lesson must contain something totally new – Shakespeare's *Romeo and Juliet* remains a great play, but even when it was written the plot was hardly original. To be creative in the maths classroom is to take the same content that has been taught for years, borrow the best ideas you can find to present them, and create a classroom experience that is tailored to the particular needs of the learners who are there at that moment. This kind of 'creative plagiarism' can lead to some of the richest learning experiences for your pupils.

SUMMARY

In this chapter you were invited to think about active and creative mathematics. The use of games as part of teaching and learning mathematics was discussed along with:

- why using games in mathematics lessons can help answer the age old question 'why are we doing this?';
- some whole class games that can be adapted to suit a wide range of topics;
- the practical aspects of using games in lessons;
- how every lesson can be seen as a story, and some can have a surprising twist at the end;
- using a mystery learning intention to focus the pupils on what they have actually been learning whilst they thought they were playing a game;
- ways of varying the pace of the lesson to maximise engagement;
- using 'spare hooks' to re-focus the lesson;
- using 'something completely different' to re-energise a lesson.

Chapter 11   Developing subject knowledge

ROBERT WARD-PENNY

Developing your subject knowledge is an important part of preparing to teach secondary mathematics. It is difficult to teach a topic well without a personal understanding of the concepts and techniques involved; teachers with secure subject knowledge are typically more confident, better at explaining ideas to pupils, and more willing to engage with questions and unplanned mathematical exploration.

Your training institution will most likely have set you targets to ensure that you are able to teach the content of examination syllabuses. These are important starting points, but a teacher's mathematical subject knowledge is something that goes beyond lists of objectives. This chapter will discuss three complementary ways in which you might challenge and extend your subject knowledge, and demonstrate how each of these can support and enhance your classroom practice.

THREE WAYS OF DEVELOPING SUBJECT KNOWLEDGE

There are many ways in which you might develop your subject knowledge throughout your teaching career. You might extend your subject knowledge:

- **higher**, by mastering some new mathematics from further on in a syllabus;
- **deeper**, by looking at the background and applications of some mathematics that you already know;
- **wider**, by learning some new mathematics from outside the syllabus.

For instance, if you already felt comfortable teaching the core content of AS-level mathematics, you might extend your subject knowledge *higher* by looking at the core content of A2-level mathematics; *deeper* by exploring some real-life applications of calculus in economics or manufacturing; or *wider* into something totally different, such as game theory. Each of these choices would support both your practice and your personal development as a mathematician in a different way.

EXTENDING YOUR SUBJECT KNOWLEDGE HIGHER

There are a number of benefits to extending your personal mathematical subject knowledge beyond the level that you are required to teach. Having a working knowledge of A-level mathematics when teaching GCSE, and of university-level mathematics when teaching A-level can not only increase your confidence, but also help you to differentiate lessons for higher attaining learners, and allow you to signpost connections and mathematical topics beyond the current syllabus.

Your training institution and placement schools will likely be able to support you in developing your subject knowledge in this direction. One common strategy is to begin by tackling an unfamiliar A-level syllabus.

Task

Briefly look over the core and applied syllabi that are currently available as part of A-level mathematics (and further mathematics). Which of these do you think you would be happy teaching at the moment? Which would you like to be comfortable teaching by the end of your training? If it is appropriate, set yourself some goals in line with your training institution's requirements.

Learning new mathematics can be challenging whilst on placement, so make sure you set yourself realistic goals. Taking some time out each week during your training will be less stressful than trying to cram an entire syllabus into one evening!

There are many ways of developing your subject knowledge 'upwards', and it is up to you to choose a way that suits you as you progress throughout your teaching career. Some teachers prefer structure, so they may choose to study an Open University module, or work towards one of the professional examinations offered by the Royal Statistical Society. Other teachers prefer a more informal approach which is more responsive to the needs of their current pupils, picking exercises out of a textbook which they find easy to use.

MATHEMATICAL THINKING

As you develop your subject knowledge 'higher', it is important also to give yourself opportunities to develop and practise your mathematical thinking. Problem-solving, investigations and mathematical recreations are just as important to you when you are learning higher-level mathematics as they are for pupils in your lessons. To this end, you might enjoy tackling the challenges posed by university admissions papers such as the STEP. Similarly, many teachers take some time once a year to see how they would have done on the Senior Mathematics Challenge run by the United Kingdom Mathematics Trust.

Task

Get hold of an old Senior Mathematics Challenge paper, either from your placement school or online (http://www.mathcomp.leeds.ac.uk/individual-competitions/senior-challenge/). Try the paper for yourself. How does the kind of mathematical thinking required here differ from an A-level paper? Might you use or adapt any of these questions to promote mathematical thinking in your A-level pupils?

EXTENDING YOUR SUBJECT KNOWLEDGE DEEPER

Another way of developing your subject knowledge is to look deeper into a topic which you already know about. Take as an example the rich topic of trigonometry, which involves lots of patterns and relationships which can be utilised to support pupils' learning.

Task

Using a calculator, find the values of tan 89, tan 89.9 and tan 89.99. What do you notice? How might sharing this pattern with pupils help them envision the idea of an asymptote on the graph of y = tan x?

Task

Using graph-plotting software or otherwise, draw the graphs of y = cos x and y = tan x with the units of the x-axis in radians. What do you notice about *how* the graphs intersect? Can you prove this? Could an A-level pupil prove this?

It is often insightful to look at some of the many applications of mathematics. Knowing how a piece of mathematics is used in a variety of situations can give you ideas for some of the starter and plenary activities described in Chapter 1, as well as providing you with an answer when your pupils ask why they might need to know about a topic. Trigonometry has a very wide range of applications, and you might be able to discuss with the pupils its use in surveying, or how it is used to rotate objects in computer graphics. You might also draw on other subjects, perhaps bringing in Snell's law from physics, or the concepts of amplitude and frequency from both physics and music. Developing your subject knowledge in this way can be the first step towards more extended cross-curricular work.

Task

Consider the following three topics: surface area, differentiation, the median. If one of your pupils asked you where these might be used in the real world, would you be able to provide an answer? Take some time now to research one of these and consolidate your answer.

One further way of adding depth to your subject knowledge is to consider the historical and cultural background of the mathematics that you are teaching. Presenting mathematics in this way can help your pupils to appreciate that mathematics has been developed by many cultures to solve authentic problems. The example of trigonometry had its origins in the work of the Babylonians and the Greeks, but the sine function as we know it originated in Indian astronomy. Indeed, the word 'sine' comes from a Sanskrit word which was translated into Arabic, then mistranslated into Latin. Trigonometry was and still is used to calculate the distances between Earth, the Sun and other planets.

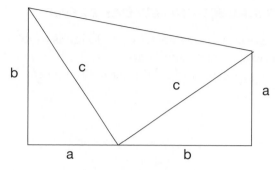

Figure 11.1 Garfield's proof of Pythagoras' theorem

The history of mathematics even includes some celebrities: Lewis Carroll and Florence Nightingale were both keen mathematicians who produced some original work. The twentieth president of the United States, James Garfield, even produced an original proof of Pythagoras' theorem. Begin with any right-angled triangle and arrange two copies as shown in Figure 11.1. Write down an expression for the area of the three resulting right-angled triangles, and equate this to an expression for the area of the trapezium. Rearrange this equation to get the familiar form of Pythagoras' theorem.

Much of this approach described in this section can be considered as building a 'general knowledge' of mathematics. Knowing about and sharing the history, purpose and oddities of mathematics with your pupils can help make the subject come to life.

Task

Choose a mathematical topic which you are likely to teach soon. Extend your subject knowledge of this topic using the questions on the prompt sheet shown in Table 11.1.

Now Try This

Once you have completed the prompt sheet, select one element which you feel would be of interest or use to your pupils. Incorporate this element into a forthcoming lesson plan; you might use it as the basis for a plenary activity, for instance, or integrate it into the main part of a lesson.

READING MATHEMATICS INTO THE WORLD

There is a great deal of value in encouraging pupils to identify mathematics in the world around them and Chapter 9 discusses ways in which you might do this. However, practising the same skill yourself is another way to add depth to your personal subject knowledge.

Instead of starting with some mathematics and looking for its application, you can begin with a real-life context and look for the mathematics involved. This starting point might be as commonplace as a traffic jam. Most of us have been frustrated at one point or another by a traffic jam which seems to have no root

Table 11.1 Deepening subject knowledge prompt sheet

Exploration • What other areas or topics in mathematics does this topic connect with? • Can this topic be drawn or illustrated using a picture or series of pictures? • Are there any patterns or mathematical coincidences related to this topic?	
Application • Which other school subjects might use this mathematical topic? How? • Which jobs might use this mathematical topic? How? • Why do you think this topic is on the syllabus?	
Context • Why and when was this topic first considered? What problem did it solve? • Which cultures were involved in the development of this topic? Did they approach it differently? • What are the origins of any vocabulary specific to this topic?	

cause, and which disappears as quickly as it arises. American mathematicians have named these events 'jamitons': self-sustained nonlinear traffic waves. The lowest traffic density at which such a jam can occur is given by the following expression:

$$\frac{\rho}{2}(1-\sqrt{1-\frac{4\beta}{u^2}})$$

where ρ is the maximum possible density of cars on the road, β is a measure of the driving conditions and drivers' behaviour, and u is the speed limit of the road. Thinking about what happens to the value of this expression as each variable is altered gives some clues as to how such traffic jams might be predicted, or even prevented. If this interests you, you could go on to research the mathematics of traffic further, exploring how mathematicians use calculus when studying traffic flow, or looking into the mathematics behind junction design.

Mathematics can equally be found in the spectacular. I was recently forwarded a video of the Kuroshio Sea, the main tank at the Okinawa Churami Aquarium in Japan. The massive scale of the tank could encourage questions about volume (it holds 7,500m³ of water), surface area and the rate at which water enters and leaves the tank. Very large and very small contexts often hold interesting mathematical opportunities.

Reading mathematics into different situations will give rise to a huge range of questions: some might be worth sharing with a class, or adapting into an activity, whilst others might be primarily for personal study. In either case, the process of creating such questions will increase your awareness of the relevance of mathematics and continue to deepen your subject knowledge.

Task

Think back over the day you have had so far, and also look around the room or space that you are in. Try to identify three objects or real-life contexts that could give rise to questions which involve A-level or undergraduate level mathematics.

EXTENDING YOUR SUBJECT KNOWLEDGE WIDER

The discussion so far has primarily focused on mathematical topics and techniques from within the syllabus. However, there is a great deal of benefit to be had from moving sideways, and exploring new topics and ideas. These can enhance and support teaching and learning, and are often quick and easy to pick up.

For instance, if you were teaching indices, you might like to show your pupils the mathematical coincidence that $2^5 \times 9^2 = 2592$. This could lead onto a discussion about *Friedman numbers*, integers which can be written as an expression using their component digits, the four basic arithmetic operations and exponentiation. The first three Friedman numbers are 25, 121 and 125. Can the pupils demonstrate why? Friedman numbers might not be on the syllabus, but they can serve as the starting point for practice and mathematical exploration.

Similarly, if you were teaching Pythagoras' theorem in three dimensions, you might look at *Euler bricks* and *perfect cuboids*. A Euler brick is a cuboid where the lengths of the edges and face diagonals are all integers. The smallest Euler brick has side lengths of 240, 117 and 44. A perfect cuboid is a Euler brick where the space diagonal is also an integer; however, at the time of writing, no-one has been able to either find a perfect cuboid or prove that such a thing is impossible. Moving sideways and sharing unsolved problems with pupils has the added benefit of demonstrating that mathematics is an active and developing discipline.

Off-syllabus mathematics can also give rise to opportunities for practising mathematical skills such as visualisation and proof. A *tetromino* is a shape made up of four squares without overlapping, and where each square shares an edge with at least one other square. There are five distinct tetrominoes, if we consider congruent reflections and rotations to be equivalent (Figure 11.2).

A little bit of trial and error might convince you that it is impossible to manoeuvre the five tetrominoes into a 4 x 5 rectangle. This result can be proved using a method called 'proof by colouring'. If you shade a 4 x 5 rectangle in the manner of a chessboard, you have 10 black and 10 white squares. However, if you colour the tetrominoes, you will end up with 11 squares of one colour, and 9 of the other. Some questions for further investigation include: how many pentominoes (made using five squares) exist, and can you prove that you haven't missed any? Can you arrange these pentominoes into a rectangle? How many tetracubes, shapes made up of four connected cubes exist?

Finally, don't forget the calendar! If you were teaching graphs close to Valentine's Day, you might use ICT to draw the graph of $(x^2 + y^2 - 1)^3 - x^2y^3 = 0$ (Figure 11.3). This piece of sideways subject knowledge could motivate GCSE pupils in their study of more basic graphs, whilst A-level pupils should be able to find the coordinates of the points where the graph crosses the axes.

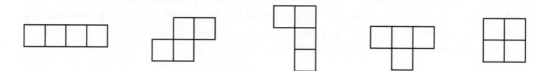

Figure 11.2 The five tetrominoes

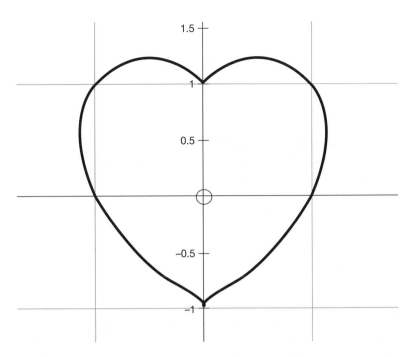

Figure 11.3 The graph of $(x^2 + y^2 - 1)^3 - x^2y^3 = 0$ drawn using Autograph

---

Task

Choose two or three of the mathematical excursions from the table below. Find out about them using the internet, reference books or otherwise.

Now Try This

Starting from one of the items you have researched, devise a starter activity or resource and go on to use it with one of your classes.

Table 11.2 Twenty 'sideways' mathematical excursions

Number Facts and Families	**Shapes, Patterns and Visualisation**
• The Hamlet Number	• Superellipses
• The Look-and-Say Sequence	• The Four Colour Theorem
• Narcissistic Numbers	• Kissing Numbers
• Bimagic Squares	• The Sierpinski Triangle
• Googols and Googolplexes	• The Tanglecube
Open Problems	**Unusual Applications**
• The Goldbach Conjecture	• Curves of Pursuit
• Catalan's Constant	• Kawasaki's Theorem
• The Happy Ending Problem	• Zipf's Law
• Ramsey Numbers	• SIR models and R_0
• The Twin Prime Conjecture	• Cellular Automata

SUPPORT AND RESOURCES

There is a fantastic range of resources currently available to support you in developing your subject knowledge in all of these directions, and many of these are online. It is impossible to provide a comprehensive list here, but three sites are listed here as starting points:

- The website 'Learn About Operational Research' (http://www.learnaboutor. co.uk) contains a number of materials which may help you move your subject knowledge higher if you are new to decision or discrete mathematics.
- The extensive reference site Wolfram Mathworld (http://mathworld. wolfram.com) is a good place to look up the unfamiliar and search out the new.
- Nrich (http://nrich.maths.org/public) offers a range of mathematical investigations for school-aged pupils which frequently step out of the standard curriculum.

The publications and websites of the Mathematical Association (http://www. m-a.org.uk/jsp/index.jsp) and the Association of Teachers of Mathematics (http:// www.atm.org.uk) are also full of ideas and resources.

Finally, there are a number of popular mathematics books written by authors such as Martin Gardner, Ian Stewart, Marcus du Sautoy and Rob Eastaway. These contain everything from mathematical puzzles to introductions to newer areas of mathematics such as knot theory and chaos theory, and offer another way to expand your subject knowledge.

CONCLUSION

Whilst subject knowledge development might not seem as pressing a goal as lesson planning or completing marking whilst on placement, it is an important element of being a secondary mathematics teacher. This chapter has argued that the goal of developing your subject knowledge is both important and manageable, as well as being a significant part of your future professional development. Continuing to explore mathematics in new ways will help to remind you of the beauty and relevance of the subject; keeping your own interest in mathematics fresh will in turn help you motivate and enthuse your pupils.

SUMMARY

In this chapter we invited you to think about the process of developing your subject knowledge and discussed a number of elements that can be used:

- considering developing your subject knowledge higher, deeper and wider;
- using enjoyable ways to challenge your mathematical thinking when extending your knowledge higher;
- extending your knowledge deeper by considering how mathematical concepts are used outside the classroom;
- deepening it further by discovering historical and cross-cultural roots;
- how sharing your deep knowledge of mathematics can make the subject come to life;
- why extending your subject knowledge wider can be useful;

- using wider knowledge to engage and interest your pupils;
- where to find resources to help you go higher, deeper and wider.

FURTHER READING

Ward-Penny, R. (2011) *Cross-Curricular Teaching and Learning in the Secondary School. . . Mathematics*, London: Routledge.

Chapter 12 Action research

Systematic reflective action to improve practice

CLARE LEE

As a teacher you may come across some issues or problems in your practice which cannot be solved simply. One part of your professional role will be to try different approaches to finding a solution, evaluating those approaches and using the results of that evaluation to inform and develop your practice. Systematic exploration of this kind is often termed 'action research'. Action research is a methodology that aims to study a social situation in order to improve circumstances for the people within that context. Action research takes many forms, but the term always indicates cycles of systematic exploration designed to solve a problem or at least improve a situation in professional practice.

You might use action research as a tool to find effective solutions for many pedagogic issues, for example you could use action research to:

- investigate the effect of using a rich task on the pupils' learning of Pythagoras' theorem;
- consider whether working together in friendship groups is more effective for your pupils than working in groups of your choosing;
- find the most effective way to get Year 8 low-attainers to learn more mathematics.

Through action research teachers become researchers in their own classrooms and can combine curriculum development and professional development in one process. The action research process is a powerful one as it provides an opportunity for both in-depth analysis and true ownership of the outcomes. Action researchers investigate something that they see as challenging and develop a solution that fits their own context and teaching.

Action research emphasises reflection on current practice and developing personal or 'living theories' (Whitehead 2008) from an analysis of that practice. The outcomes of such research are both personal and practical. However, you will often come across other teachers sharing their experiences and discoveries in school magazines or teaching journals, for example *Mathematics Teaching* (ATM) or *Mathematics in School* (MA). In this way the ideas that are generated can be made available for other practitioners to think about incorporating into their own practice.

Action research may be defined as '*the study of a social situation with a view to improving the quality of the action within it.*' It aims to feed on practical judgement in concrete situations, and the validity of the 'theories' or hypotheses it generates depends not so much on 'scientific' tests of truth as on their usefulness in helping people to act more intelligently and skilfully.

(Elliott 1991, p. 69; his emphasis)

SMALL CHANGES CAN MAKE A BIG DIFFERENCE

Engaging in an action research project usually involves exploring a discrete and often small aspect of teaching and learning. However, even at this scale, the process encourages teachers to become more reflective about their own practice and it can therefore enable some teachers to make dramatic improvements in their teaching. Since each teacher decides his or her own research focus related to some real practical concern, action research questions take the form of:

the commonplace, fundamentally crucial questions of, . . . 'How am I going to improve the process of education for myself and my children?'

(McNiff 1988, p. xvi)

Professor Tim Brighouse talks about the impact of what he terms 'butterflies' on the everyday life of the school and on the process of school improvement. He defines butterflies as 'those small interventions that have a disproportionate effect on meaning and change' (Brighouse and Woods 1999, p. 80). The concept of the 'butterfly effect' has been taken from ideas around 'chaos theory', where very small changes can produce massive effects. In his book *How to Improve Your School* (Brighouse and Woods 1999), Brighouse provides as an example butterflies stirring the air in Peking that within a month transform into storm systems in New York.

Task

Think of a small change that has made a big difference to you or your teaching. This could be a different way of studying that helped you learn more or a difference in the way that you approach teaching which made your lessons more successful.

ACTION RESEARCH CYCLES

Action research is always open ended. It begins with an idea that you want to develop, or a problem that you encounter that turns into a question of the form 'How do I . . .?' or 'If I . . . then . . .?' Action research is, then, the developmental process of researching practice and finding potential ideas that may form answers, putting an idea into practice, investigating how well that idea answers the problem, and continually checking whether what is happening is in line with what you wish to happen. Seen in this way, action research is a form of cyclical self evaluation.

Action research is simply a form of self-reflective enquiry undertaken by participants in social situations in order to improve the rationality and justice of their own practices, their understanding of these practices, and the situations in which the practices are carried out.

(Carr and Kemmis 1986, p. 162)

For example,

- If you use a rich task to introduce Pythagoras' theorem you may find on evaluation that the pupils remember how to use that theorem very well. Therefore you may decide to use rich tasks in another learning episode and investigate whether that is as effective.
- If you try to improve Year 8 low-attainers' learning by asking them to sit and work individually, you may find on evaluation that the atmosphere in the class seems poor. You may now decide to try asking them to work in pairs of your choosing; subsequently you may look at the tasks they are working on.

At each stage of the action research cycle it is possible to act alone. However, working collaboratively can enhance each phase. It is easier to ask and answer hard questions when working in a small group. Discussion can help establish the full meaning of a situation and provide motivation to look in-depth at the evidence. Other people can provide ideas to improve the plans. In sharing research, teachers create a 'thinking culture', exploring more fully the complexities of teaching and learning.

THE ACTION RESEARCH CYCLE

Action research can be summed up as systematically exploring a change in classroom practice, applying research cycles in order to know that an improvement has occurred and sharing that experience with others.

An action research sequence

- *review current practice*: you could use the monitoring and evaluation of lessons and sequences of lessons that is part of your day-to-day practice to do this;
- *identify an aspect* that you want to investigate;

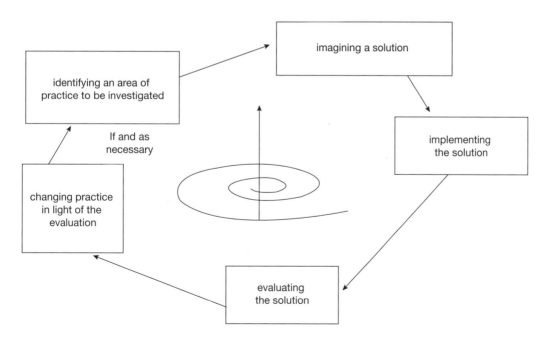

Figure 12.1 The action research cycle. Adapted from http://www.jeanmcniff.com/booklet 1.html

- *imagine a way forward*: reading teaching journals, exploring the web and especially working with others are good ways of doing this;
- *form the problem* and imagined solution into a research question;
- *try out* the imagined solution; and
- *evaluate what happens*: seeking evidence to support what you see as happening and possibly involving others in the discussion of the outcomes of your innovation;
- *modify your practice* in the light of what you have found, and continuing working in this new way or trying another option if the innovation did not provide a complete answer;
- *monitor* the new idea;
- *review and evaluate* the modified action and so on . . .

A simplified version of this sequence is given in Table 12.1.

Action research (as its name suggests) requires both action and ideas more traditionally associated with research. Therefore, engaging in action research not only requires you to use existing evaluation approaches and hunches about your teaching to decide on the problem to tackle, it also asks you to read what others have said on the subject, where others have found problems and what solutions they have found. It asks you to try out some innovation in your practice but also asks that you consider why that innovation might work, look at assumptions that

Table 12.1 An action research cycle

Look →	Think →	Act →	Reflect
Forming a **picture** by scrutinising evidence about what is currently happening. The idea becomes a **question** and the problem is defined and described. **Information** is gained from articles and books.	The problem has been defined and evidence has been found about other approaches. Now is the time to **think** about and **imagine** the approach to take in solving the problem and what a successful outcome will look like.	Put the ideas into practice.	What has worked well and what still needs improvement?

Table 12.2 The action research balancing act

Good action research balances:

Lots of action	with	Lots of research
Information driven		Knowledge driven
Observation		Engaging with the research community
Trying out something		Conceptualising and theorising
Experiential		Identifying assumptions
Knowing about		About understanding practice

you or others may have previously made and thus reach a deeper understanding of the solution you seek. You will not just report that the pupils seem to enjoy the new lessons, but you will also seek evidence to back up your hunches and thereby allow you to be sure 'what works' and what could still be improved.

DESIGNING YOUR ACTION RESEARCH PROJECT

Identifying the focus of your study may be quite difficult when you start teaching, as you will want to know about many aspects of your practice and may think that everything needs improvement! Remember that action research is about your own professional development and therefore you will want to study something that interests you.

Imagine the change

Your action research project is not just about identifying a problem – it is also about trying out ideas that may help to solve that problem. Once you have settled on what you want to change in your teaching, you will have to start thinking about or imagining how that change could be brought about. This will almost certainly involve you in discussions with other people, but also in reading books about possible solutions or searching the web for ideas. You should spend some time on imagining solutions and making plans for implementation, as this can save you from making mistakes or running up against unforeseen problems. However, if all teachers were able to implement innovations without any unforeseen problems there would be no need for action research.

You may want to investigate something straightforward such as 'What happens if I tell one class not to put their hands up to answer a question and I choose who answers the question?' This is simple because it is one action with one class; however, after the first try out it may become more complex. How do I choose who answers? How do I devise questions that are worth thinking about and discussing the way that 'no hands up' encourages? Thus the cycles of action research begin.

Or you may want to start with a more complex innovation, such as working in a way that encourages a class to develop more complex thinking skills. This will require detailed planning before you start: for example you will need to ask 'What complex thinking skills do I want the class to develop?'; 'What ideas already exist to introduce these skills?'; 'How do I encourage the learning of mathematics alongside these thinking skills?' and 'What aspect of the curriculum will lend itself to working in this way?' All of these questions can be thought about in the planning stage, but the action research will provide the evidence that makes the answers compelling.

Ask the question

It is usually a good idea to devise a question to answer at the start of your action research project. This way you will know at the end of the first cycle if you have completely answered the question or whether there is more research to be done to provide an answer. Therefore, the best question is the one that will lead you to look at your practice deeply and engage in cycles of continuous learning from your everyday experience.

Questions can be stated in an 'if/then' format. For example:

- If I [insert the action to be taken], then how will it affect [describe one or more possible consequences of the action]?
- If I use a 'no hands up to answer a question' rule, then how will it affect the number of students actively engaged in answering questions?
- If I focus on complex thinking skills, then how will it affect the students' ability to answer harder examination questions?

The question should be clear about both what the researcher intends to do and what the possible outcomes might be.

Decide what success will look like

It is important at this time to think about what you expect to happen. This has similarities to setting out success criteria in lessons. Identify at the start of the process what you hope to achieve by implementing your ideas, then you will know if and when you have been successful.

> **Task**
>
> Think about an aspect of your practice that you have found problematic and make a brief search in this volume for solutions to that problem. Form the problem and potential solution into a research question. Now imagine what a successful answer to that problem might be. What could you do that you do not currently do? What difference would this solution make to the pupils?

Collect the evidence

Since it is your research project, the only person you really have to convince of the efficacy of your innovation is yourself, although reporting on your project at a department meeting may be useful. However, it can be difficult to convince even yourself about how well an innovation worked, so you will need to decide on what data to collect and how to do this. Video can be useful as it is possible to watch the recording several times and begin to understand such things as how your actions affected the pupils and vice versa. However, there can be drawbacks: not all pupils will consent to being filmed and you must get at least the permission of the head teacher before you video, even if you do not intend to show the video to anyone else. If you do intend to show it to, for example, your fellow teachers, you will need written permission from parents.

Interviews with pupils can be useful, but time consuming. You may need to ask pupils to be interviewed during their breaks, as taking lesson time could disadvantage those pupils that you interview. Interviewing is also a skill that needs to be practised. If you audio-record the interviews you may find that you do most of the talking. Plan for this by preparing the questions you will ask and interview pupils in twos or threes so that the atmosphere is more like a conversation.

Most other forms of data can be collected in the general course of your teaching, provided you plan first, for example homework or other written work in class. You may decide to use a test at the start of the project (pre-test) and one at the end (post-test), although all test data must be treated with caution. For example, if the tests are different, are you sure they are of comparable difficulty? If the same test is used, are you sure any improvement is directly attributable to the innovation?

Reflect on your data

Once you have tried out your innovation and collected evidence about how well your actions addressed the specific problem, the next stage is to reflect on the evidence that you have. Again, reflection must be systematic; it can be easy to say it was all wonderful because the pupils enjoyed themselves, but then the question is did they learn any mathematics? However, as a beginning teacher, it is more likely that you will be hypercritical, perhaps by saying that the pupils were too noisy when they were excited by working in a different way. Neither way is the best.

If you set out your criteria for success carefully at the start of your project then they will guide your reflection. How far did you achieve your criteria? Did everyone in the class learn the same thing? Did some learn better than others? Did the normally taciturn girl answer some questions? Did the activities encourage a thinking atmosphere?

A useful reflection tool can be to think about the innovation from different points of view. What was the effect on the girl who usually takes everything in her stride, was she able to challenge herself? What about the boy who makes a lot of mistakes, was he able to learn from his mistakes? What about the pupils who usually do very little because they say that they are 'stuck' – were they able to get on more purposefully?

Remember to include your own point of view and that of any other adults in the room so that the conclusions you reach about the efficacy of the innovation include everyone. It can also be very useful to involve other people in the reflection process. Their view on the data will be less intimate and therefore they can give you another valid view, and ideas come out in conversation with others that just do not occur to you when you view the data by yourself. The other people that you involve could be friends, other teachers or perhaps your mentor or head of department. It is the different perspectives that are so valuable not necessarily the levels of experience.

Task

Think about the question that you devised in the previous task and the success criteria you decided on.

- Now consider what data you could collect to enable you to know how successful your solution will be.
- Think about how best to reflect on this data. Whose viewpoint will be vital to take into account? What will tell you most about the success of the change in practice?

Do your answers to this task make you want to change your success criteria or the data you set out to collect? It often happens that when you consider different viewpoints, your ideas about success criteria change as well, which indicates why the whole action research process needs to be thought through before you start.

Decide on where next

The last part of each cycle of action research is to decide what you have learned by completing the process and to consider what to do next. It may be that the next step is to continue with the same idea, enabling both your pupils and yourself to become more used to acting in a certain way and for your innovation to become embedded in your practice. Alternatively, it may be that the ideas need tweaking and that a further cycle of the research process is needed to establish whether the tweaks are the right ones.

It is very unlikely that you will have completely solved the particular problem that you were seeking a solution to in the first cycle of research and most action research projects require two or three cycles to provide the answers that are sought. Hence it is worth planning for more than one cycle when you begin.

Now Try This

Use the ideas in this chapter to solve a problem that you have encountered in teaching. Make sure the issue is important to you and use the ideas about systematic enquiry to come up with an approach that works for you.

ACTION RESEARCH AND PROFESSIONAL DEVELOPMENT

Action research can be an important part of your professional development because of its potential to tackle and find solutions for issues that are personal to you. The whole process is about becoming a better teacher and enabling your pupils to learn mathematics more effectively and hence it is particularly powerful for professional development. If you engage in an action research project, not only will you find a solution to a problem but you will also understand why it is the best solution for you, and you will be able to articulate the reasoning behind acting in that way. Therefore you will be in a position to share your experiences with others and possibly help them to fit your solution to their context.

As has been indicated throughout this chapter, many of the most successful action research projects are completed by groups of teachers. If you work in a group of two or three you can plan together and come up with compelling solutions. You can also help one another collect data and reflect on that data. It is so much easier to see the effective practice when looking at someone else's lesson than when considering your own.

Some mathematics departments have begun to use their 'in-school training days' to work together to plan an action research project in order to implement an innovation in the curriculum or in pedagogy. The sense of purposeful systematic effort engendered by the action research process will result in the best way of implementing the innovation for the department and will help the department develop a sense of working together for the good of the department and the pupils in their care. This is professional development in action.

SUMMARY

In this chapter you have been introduced to the concept of action research as a means of solving problems that you will encounter in your teaching career. The discussion included the following:

- what action research methodology is;
- defining your idea as a research question;
- the action research cycle;
- designing a project and putting the ideas of action research into practice;
- the part that action research can play in professional development.

FURTHER READING

Hopkins, D. (2002) *A Teacher's Guide to Classroom Research*, Maidenhead: Open University Press.

McNiff, J. (n.d.) 'Action research for professional development: concise advice for new action researchers', available from http://www.jeanmcniff.com/ar-booklet.asp

Websites and resources

Audacity – a freely available audio editing programme
http://audacity.sourceforge.net/download/

Autograph – dynamic graphing software
http://www.autograph-math.com/

ATM – Association of Teachers of Mathematics
http://www.atm.org.uk/

Cabri – dynamic geometry programme
http://www.cabri.com/

Census at School
http://www.censusatschool.org.uk/

Countdown Numbers Game
The author can be contacted on CSfarmer@CSFsoftware.co.uk

Exam Solutions providing recordings of solutions to examination questions
http://www.examsolutions.co.uk

Fourbidden Card game
The game can be purchased at: http://www.atm.org.uk/shop/products/act013.html

Gapminder – an interactive tool for displaying statistical information and trends
http://www.gapminder.org/

Geogebra – freely available dynamic geometry and graphing software
http://www.geogebra.org

Geometer's Sketchpad – dynamic graphing software
http://www.dynamicgeometry.com/

Jing – a recorder for use with an IWB
http://www.techsmith.com/jing.html

Learn about Operational Research
http://www.learnaboutor.co.uk

Mathcomp – Senior Maths Challenge paper
http://www.mathcomp.leeds.ac.uk/individual-competitions/senior-challenge/

MA – Mathematical Association
http://www.m-a.org.uk/jsp/index.jsp

Maths 4 Real – Channel 4 Learning
http://www.channel4learning.com/index.html

Mathsnet
http://www.mathsnet.net

Mathswatch providing screen shot solutions to mathematical problems
http://www.mathswatch.co.uk

Mcniff, Jean – guidance on action research
http://www.jeanmcniff.com/ar-booklet.asp

National Centre for Excellence in the Teaching of Mathematics
https://www.ncetm.org.uk/resources/31033

NRich – many rich tasks and some dynamic learning environments
http://nrich.maths.org

Prezi – presentation software
http://prezi.com

Promethean whiteboards
http://www.prometheanworld.com/en-gb

Scratch – a programming language
http://scratch.mit.edu/

Screencast-O-Matic – an on-line recorder for use with an IWB
http:// www.screencast-o-matic.com

SMARTboard whiteboards
http://www.smarttech.com/gb

Standards Unit – Improving learning in Mathematics; collaborative learning resources containing many rich and interesting learning materials
http://www.nationalstemcentre.org.uk/elibrary/collection/291/materials

Tarsia software
http://download.cnet.com/Formulator-Tarsia/3000–2051_4–10584458.html

Trevor Fletcher films
http://www.atm.org.uk/resources/films.html

Wolfram Mathworld
http://mathworld.wolfram.com/

YouTube
http://www.youtube.co.uk

References

Ahmed, A, (Project director) (1987) *Better Mathematics,* London: HMSO.

ATM (2004) *Thinkers,* Derby: Association of Teachers of Mathematics (ATM).

BECTA (2007) Harnessing Technology Schools Survey, available online at http://collection. europarchive.org/tna/20040722012352/http://partners.becta.org.uk/upload-dir/downloads/page_documents/research/harnessing_technology_schools_survey07. pdf.

Black, P., Harrison, C., Lee, C., Marshall, B. and Wiliam, D. (2004) *Working Inside the Black Box,* London: GL Assessment.

Brighouse, T. and Woods, D. (1999) *How to Improve Your School,* London: Routledge.

Carr, W. and Kemmis, S. (1986*) Becoming Critical: Education, Knowledge, and Action Research,* London: Routledge Farmer.

Clark-Wilson, A., Oldknow, A. and Sutherland, R. (2011) *Digital Technologies and Mathematics Education,* London: Joint Mathematical Council. Available online at: http://bit.ly/jmcdt report.

Cockcroft, W. (1982) *Mathematics Counts,* London: HMSO.

DCSF (2008) *Assessing Pupils' Progress in Mathematics at Key Stage 3,* London: DCSF.

DfES (2005) Standards Unit. Available online at: http://tlp.excellencegateway.org.uk/ teachingandlearning/downloads/default.aspx#/math_learning.

Dubin, P. (1962) *Human Relations in Administration,* Englewood Cliffs, NJ: Prentice Hall.

Elliot, J. (1991) *Action Research for Educational Change,* Buckingham: Open University Press.

Foster, C. (2010) *Resources for Teaching Mathematics,* London: Continuum.

French, D. and Strip, C. (eds) (1997) *'Pig' and Other Tales: A Book of Mathematical Readings,* Leicester: Mathematical Association.

Gardner, M. (2006) *Aha! A Two Volume Collection: Aha! Gotcha, Aha! Insight,* Washington DC: The Mathematical Association of America.

Gartner, A., Conway Kohler, M. And Riessman, F. (1971) *Children Teach Children: Learning by Teaching,* New York: Harper & Row.

Goodlad, S. and Hirst, B. (1989) *Peer Tutoring: A Guide to Learning by Teaching,* London: Routledge & Kegan Paul.

Henning, J. (2008) *The Art of Discussion-Based Teaching: Opening up Conversation in the Classroom.* New York and London: Routledge.

HMI (1985) *Mathematics from 5 to 16,* London: HMSO.

Hopkins, D. (2002) *A Teacher's Guide to Classroom Research,* Maidenhead, UK: Open University Press.

Lee, C. (2006) *Language for Learning Mathematics: Assessment for Learning in Practice,* Maidenhead, UK: Open University Press.

Martin, C. (2011) *Big Ideas,* Derby: Association of Teachers of Mathematics (ATM).

McNiff, J. (1988) *Action Research: Principles and Practice* (First Edition). Basingstoke: Macmillan.

Mercer, N. (2000) *Words and Minds: How We Use Language to Think Together,* London and New York: Routledge.

Mercer, N. and Littleton, K. (2007) *Dialogue and the Development of Children's Thinking: A Sociocultural Approach,* London: Routledge.

Miller, D., Glover, D. and Averis, D. (2008) *Enabling Enhanced Mathematics Teaching with Interactive Whiteboards,* Final Report for the National Centre for Excellence in the Teaching of Mathematics, Keele University, Keele. Available at: http://bit.ly/iwbreport.

National Centre for Excellence in the Teaching of Mathematics (2010) *Mathematics and Digital Technologies: New Beginnings,* London: National Centre for Excellence in the Teaching of Mathematics.

National Curriculum Council (1989) *Mathematics: Non-Statutory Guidance,* York: NCC.

OfSTED (2008) *Mathematics: Understanding the Score,* London: HMSO. Available at: http://bit.ly/ofstedmmscore.

Oldknow, A. and Knights, C. (2011) *Mathematics Education with Digital Technology,* London: Continuum.

Ollerton, M. (2002) *Learning and Teaching Mathematics Without a Textbook,* Derby: Association of Teachers of Mathematics (ATM).

Ollerton, M. and Watson, A. (2001) *Inclusive Mathematics,* London: Continuum.

Ollerton, M. and Watson, A. (2007) *GCSE Coursework in Mathematics,* MT203, Derby: Association of Teachers of Mathematics (ATM).

Perrenoud, P. (1998) 'From formative evaluation to a controlled regulation of learning', *Assessment in Education: Principles, Policy and Practice,* 5 (1): 85–103.

Stigler, J. and Hiebert, J. (2009) *The Teaching Gap,* New York: Free Press.

Swan, M. (2006) *Collaborative Learning in Mathematics: A Challenge to Our Beliefs and Practices,* Leicester: National Institute of Adult Continuing Education.

Ward-Penny, R. (2011) *Cross-Curricular Teaching and Learning in the Secondary School . . . Mathematics,* London: Routledge.

Whitehead, J. (2008) 'Using a living theory methodology in improving practice and generating educational knowledge in living theories', *Educational Journal of Living Theories,* 1(1): 103–26.

Index